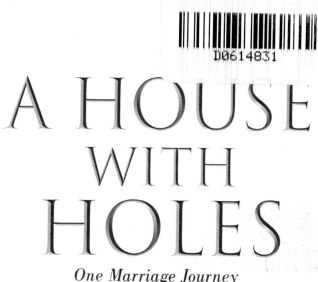

A HOUSE
WITH
HOLES

*One Marriage Journey
in a Charleston Renovation*

A HOUSE
WITH
HOLES

*One Marriage Journey
in a Charleston Renovation*

DENISE MAST BROADWATER

Foreword by Shannon Ethridge, MA

MOUNTAIN VIEW PRESS

Published by Mountain View Press, an imprint of Redemption Press, 1730 Railroad Street, Enumclaw, WA 98022. (360) 226-3488

www.mountainviewpress.com

Mountain View Press is honored to present this title in partnership with the author. The views expressed or implied in this work are those of the author. Mountain View Press provides our imprint seal representing design excellence, creative content, and high-quality production.

Sketch of Charleston Cottage by Jessica Roux. Used with permission.

ISBN softcover: 978-1-951350-00-0
ISBN hardcover: 978-1-951350-01-7
ISBN ePub: 978-1-951350-02-4
ISBN Mobi: 978-1-951350-03-1

Library of Congress Catalog Card Number: 2019910491

DEDICATION

For Greg,
my husband and my brightest life-light.
Your gifts are extraordinary,
and there's no one I'd rather work alongside.
Thanks for changing our lives
and supporting me to change mine.

TABLE OF CONTENTS

FOREWORD

When we take on a big building project, we can usually assume that it will require:

- more TIME than we allotted
- more ENERGY than we expected
- more MONEY than we had budgeted

I learned all of these truths the hard way many years ago, when we moved from the hustle and bustle of Dallas to the serene piney woods of east Texas.

We found a secluded 122 acres with a cute little log cabin overlooking a huge stocked pond. It was idyllic, except that the doctor who had previously owned this home away from home had died ten years earlier, and his family hadn't returned since. Imagine ten years of dust, cobwebs, and even a few dead mice and snakeskins, and you'll know what we first encountered! When my mother walked in, she started crying. "You've just got so much work to do here!" she bemoaned.

But the overwhelming projects didn't deter us. We saw our cabin as a diamond in the rough that just needed polishing. A *lot* of polishing.

With a family of four, we knew we'd eventually

need to add on to the 1,700-square-foot cabin to make it comfortable for the long term, but we wanted to wait until we could really do it right. We lived in it for seven years before we began the massive add-on project, which would give us a total of 4,500 square feet. Yes, we practically built a whole new house—which just happened to be right next door to the old one!

We had to pay extra attention to make sure that everything blended just right. Whatever materials we used in the new construction, such as decorative fieldstone and prairie-mutton windows, we also added to the original structure, for uniformity. And we paid master craftsmen to take chisels and chains to the new log beams to "age" them so that they looked approximately the same age as the ones on the original side of the house. I kept thinking, *We sure are paying a LOT of money to make something so new look so old!* But imagine my delight when newcomers to our home had to ask, "So which is the *old side* and which is the *new side?*"

From planning to completion, the project took a total of three years. There were a lot of unexpected twists and turns, the biggest of which was the day we were meeting with the builder to go over the budget. He presented his itemized list of material costs and labor, and we were flabbergasted at the bid! Immediately, my eyes scanned the pages, trying to identify a way to cut some major corners.

"Do we really need to spend *that* much money on the new foundation?" I asked naively. It was almost a third of the budget! But before our builder had a chance to answer, my mind flashed back to a moment in history that I'll never forget . . .

I was baking a pineapple upside-down cake for my grandfather's birthday, and I was ready to turn it over onto a cookie sheet to let it cool. However, I could find no cookie sheets in my cupboards. It hit me that my daughter had taken them to her kindergarten classroom for a science project. I had to improvise, so the best I could come up with was a wire cooling rack, which I covered in aluminum foil. I was pretty proud of myself . . . until I got to the nursing home and realized that the cake was now "rippled" from one end to the other, like a Ruffles potato chip. Because it didn't have a firm foundation to rest upon, sections sank through the cracks of the wire rack.

I snapped back to reality. *I don't want our new house falling through any foundation cracks like that birthday cake did!* My builder confirmed my suspicion as he declared unapologetically, "Ma'am, if you're going to cut corners, I certainly *don't* recommend that it be in the foundation work!"

Fast-forward a few years later to 2009. I began developing a twelve-month online course for aspiring writers and speakers—The B.L.A.S.T. Mentorship Program (B.L.A.S.T. being an acronym for Building Leaders, Authors, Speakers & Teachers). As I laid out the overall concepts I wanted to teach my B.L.A.S.T. participants, I realized that "building" anything requires similar strategies—visionary thinking, careful planning, smart budgeting, creative processes, etc.

 xi

Therefore I used the architectural blueprint analogy throughout the materials to coach people through the process of building their own speaking and writing platforms.

So imagine my delight when I meet Denise Broadwater, a professional counselor who is looking to write her own book about building healthier relationships using the analogy of her own major home renovation! We were kindred spirits from the start, and watching Denise get traction with her vision to bring this book to life has been an absolute *joy*! I also had the privilege of coaching her through a four-day "B.L.A.S.T. Next Level" experience, where she presented her proposed book ideas to the entire group, and I watched everyone light up with great anticipation!

Denise's heart for helping others absolutely *shines*, and her wisdom runs *deep* based on her own unique life experiences as a wife, mom, counselor, and friend. Denise understands that relationships *are* a lot like house renovations. They *do* take a lot more time, energy, and resources than we can fathom. But she also knows that cutting corners on foundational truths and principles is incredibly detrimental in the long run and that there is no greater, more rewarding investment than to build something absolutely beautiful *together*.

So if you're looking for a great read that will help you develop a realistic vision for a happier, healthier home environment—not just because of the lovely exterior renovations but because of the rich relationships contained therein —then you've picked up the right book! May you be inspired to cherish the opportunities you have to create something beautiful in your own home, life, marriage, and family!

~ Shannon Ethridge, MA
Life/relationship coach, speaker, and author of twenty-two
books, including the million-copy best-selling
Every Woman's Battle series.

$\mathcal{A}$s I STOOD AT THE stove, I glimpsed movement out of the corner of my eye. I looked over my shoulder and saw the gray-brown bushy tail of a raccoon moving slowly away through the plastic curtain into the construction area.

I shut off the stove, stuck the soup pot into the warm oven, and slammed the door behind me as I fled into the front room. My first impulse was to fire off an angry text to Greg, but I knew I'd regret what I would write in my current emotional state.

Instead, I trembled on the bed with a blanket over me. The longer I waited, the more I felt sorry for myself. How much of this was I supposed to stand?

Acknowledgments

Many thanks to Donna Brannon, a bestie who pushed me to write my story before I believed I could, who puts me to the test, and I love her for it.

My editor, Lana McAra, who smoothed out all the rough edges. Beyond the love of writing, we share DNA. Thanks for all you did to make my story shine in this debut book.

Dr. Larry Wagner, professor of marriage and family therapy at Columbia International University whose training in marriage theory is foundational to my counseling. While it has altered slightly during my years of treatment, I still value his perspective and use his practical helps.

Connie Gonzalez, Ruthie Cooper, Jill Broadwater, Axa Carnes and Marci Cairns, my personal cheerleaders. Thanks for allowing me to bounce ideas off you, for reading and proofing, and most of all, for giving of your time to this project.

BLAST NEXT 2018 ladies: Alicea Davis, Dena Johnson Martin, Loyla Louvis, Laura White, Phylis Mantelli, Carol Larson, Tamara Denis-Lewis, and Sandra Lovelace—all beautiful, impactful women walking this life with me. You get it in ways few others do. And Shannon Ethridge, who brought us together in the first place.

Thanks to Mick Silva, my writing coach, who was the first to believe in the potential of my scribbles.

And thanks to my mother, Betty Laughter, who may never know her true part in this work and the works to come.

Chapter 1

A BRICK FOR CHRISTMAS

*L*INED UP LIKE A BASTION along the bay, Charleston's parade of historic homes dates back to the 1600s—some of the first structures built in this country. Preserving this rich past has a cult following here. Locals cry out if scavengers collect relics from their sacred lands. They resent poachers. *Do not disturb* is the local mantra, touted on signs, bumper stickers, and badges with slogans like, "Gut fish, not houses." Local ordinances within the hallowed peninsula forbid a house to be torn down. Houses are to be preserved and respectfully renovated.

Charleston culture pushes to save its history and keep it for the enjoyment of all. On a recent carriage tour, our docent pointed out a street that looks just as it did in the 1700s, so much so that movie makers often film on that street. The city draws millions of visitors each year, people who long for simpler, more primitive times.

This is the environment we chose for our renovation. As glamorous as I envisioned owning a part of this history would be, reality hit when more primitive times showed up as renovation dust, cooking meals on a hot plate, and icy drafts.

Our second winter in Charleston began with cold seeping in by mid-December. Although winter in Charleston is mild compared to most of the country, our blood ran thin because we were used to the warmer climate. As the damp cold crept into the house, my bones felt saturated with it. I was cold through and through.

Greg set the vent-free heater in front of the fireplace. The unit was rated for more than our small area, yet the heat pooled in the center of the room, and the corners stayed frigid. Greg did some research and spent a Saturday morning sealing the windows with a plastic film to keep out the drafts, but the lack of insulation in the walls made plugging the holes around the doors and windows futile. We were in a losing battle until our walls were redone.

I wonder how the poor dears from years past lived in this house under these conditions. It takes me back to tent camping with friends and family in the Appalachian Mountains, where we huddled near a central campfire before climbing into our cold tents for the night, praying our zero-rated sleeping bags would use our body heat to warm us. Warm clothing, wool socks, and lots of hot chocolate were our only recourse. I go back to these defenses, putting on my warmest PJ's, hiding under a down comforter, and reading my latest obsession.

Greg could not do the mechanical part of this

project himself because he didn't have a license. Finding a company Greg could trust to do the job to his specifications slowed everything down. So, there we were, coming up on Christmas with little more than a gas heater. I voiced my complaints, but I was forced to accept my discomfort as part of living in a project while working on it.

Living through these stages of renovation broke me down in some ways. What I thought I needed to make my life work became peripheral. A life unencumbered was freedom. I was still in the process of releasing things. From time to time, the pressure built in me, and Greg faced the brunt of my frustration. That afternoon, after coming in from a long week, I began dinner on my hot plate in our front room retreat. As Greg came onto the piazza, I started in with my attitude.

"I am done. I need central heat, a washer, dryer, and a floor that can be mopped. The dust is constant." When he didn't respond, my voice rose. "Are you listening?"

"I don't like it when you say *done*, Denise. I know it's taking forever. Are you done with me? Do I get lumped in with the house?"

"Well . . . I guess I'll keep you." I managed an upside-down smile. "I guess I am saying just ditch the house because I would want you to come with me."

"And just where would we go? This is our only home and friends would tire of us staying over." Charleston's rent district was so expensive that managing it along with costly renovations was just out of the question.

We both laughed and tried to come to terms with where we stood. It wasn't even half complete, and the worst may be ahead of us. But the things left are amenities we took for granted in the past, like heat.

This no-closet, dust-filled cottage on the upper West Side of Charleston pinged me from time to time, but I consoled myself knowing life was short and each day a gift. I rested in the belief that this project would one day end. My only choice was to struggle through.

This was the second Christmas season without a family celebration at our house. Before, most years I loved to host a number of Christmas parties and family gatherings. Christmas was my favorite time to show love and appreciation for people who blessed us through the year. My gift of hospitality was on hold indefinitely. I missed that part of myself.

My adult children arranged to have our gathering at our eldest son's home, making the holidays manageable. I tried to be content with being together as a family and not give into the longing to have my children sit at my table for Christmas dinner. This time of year confirmed more and more that our family home was no more.

After dinner, I generally retired to the front room where I would sit with my laptop and pour out written words, scan social media, and catch up on emails. But this particular evening, about a week before leaving for the holidays, I felt too cold to type. Instead I put on my thickest pajamas and snuggled in my bed. Greg was stretched out on the sectional in the living room, reading with a TV show going for background noise.

Suddenly, a blast shook the side of the house. Glass shattered, and I heard a heavy thud. In my dreamlike state, I assumed a gunshot tore through the house.

I bolted upright. "Greg! Are you OK?" I desperately prayed that Greg wasn't bleeding. My active imagination anticipated a horror scene outside my bedroom door.

Greg called back. "I am good. Don't come in here, Denise. Glass is everywhere!"

I glided to the door with one catlike movement, afraid to look, afraid of what I would see. Slowly opening the door of our makeshift wall, I peeked out.

Greg was down on all fours. A brick lay inside the original mullioned window, and glass particles spread throughout the room. Greg inspected the floor for any evidence of what might have happened.

"That brick came through the window?" I pointed to the broken pane next to the front door.

Still looking at the floor, Greg said, "I was sound asleep on the sectional sofa when it happened." He looked up at me. "Thank God, Denise, you weren't sitting there because it could have hit you in the head."

My heart raced up to another level. My breath caught in my throat. I trembled as I had a flashback from middle school when a group of bullies slapped me around for not setting up a volleyball spike.

Greg and I were being targeted. It was the only explanation.

As I came to my senses to peruse the damage,

I tried to console myself by looking at the bright side—this old six-paned window was soon to be replaced. One small section had shattered. Other than that, little else was hurt.

I grabbed my phone off the nightstand. "I am calling the police to report this."

Greg doesn't like confrontation or dealing with the police. He walked into the other room with little more than, "OK." He knew any attempt to keep me from calling was a losing battle.

In seconds, the operator was on the line. "911. What is your emergency?"

"We had a brick thrown through our porch window about five minutes ago."

"I am so sorry for your trouble this evening, ma'am. Is anyone hurt? Do you need me to dispatch EMS?"

"No. Fortunately no one was in the path of the brick, but we need someone to investigate and advise us on how to proceed. I'm scared the person may be outside."

"Stay inside your house until the officers arrive. They are in route now and should be there shortly. Please stay on the line with me until they arrive."

I awkwardly held the phone to my ear. Tears formed in my eyes. Sometimes I had to wonder if our dedication to this project was worth what we faced in the two years since we moved here. Was this brick a warning, telling us to get out of the neighborhood? Were we invading a place where we were not wanted? But our neighbors were so friendly. Nothing made sense.

I looked for Greg to get his thoughts on the situation. He was in the back of the house getting a broom and dustpan to finish cleaning up the glass.

"Who would do such a thing? This makes me so uneasy."

"Let's talk to the police when they come. They are more aware of the calls and this type of behavior in the area than we are. Maybe they'll step up patrols and give us advice."

The policeman arrived and surveyed the damage. Short and wide with his blond hair in a marine cut, he shined his giant flashlight under our porch and examined the backyard.

In a moment, he came to our door. "I am sure this is a bit unnerving for you folks tonight," he said, all business.

Greg said, "This has gone to the point that my wife thought we might need things checked on out here."

Me: Damsel in Distress. Greg: Macho Man who was only calming the wife.

After examining the brick on the living room floor, the policeman told us it came from our own courtyard.

"Mr. Broadwater," he stared down at his pad, writing notes as he spoke, "do you have any form of protection in your house should someone try to force their way inside to steal or harm you or your wife?"

Greg and I looked at each other, shocked. We had forgotten the Stand Your Ground protections afforded here in the South. We decided to not answer that question.

"I work these streets," he went on, "and I don't think it is out of hate or malice. Maybe it's some teens who are out of school on Christmas break, and they were horsing around out here. Just to be safe, having a form of protection would be wise." He tore off a copy of the page and handed it to Greg. "I can write you a report for your homeowners insurance, if you need it."

"No need, Officer," Greg said, folding the paper. "I'm going to have that glass pane fixed in just a few minutes. I won't need to file a claim. Thank you for coming out to check on us."

Before he left, the policeman pointed out the loose bricks under the edge of our piazza. "Get rid of these bricks and keep your gate closed." The officer kicked at the bricks stacked next to our porch step. "I know it is not a total fix for this mischief, but we don't want to provide their ammunition, if you know what I mean."

"I'll get those right away," Greg respectfully responded.

"Here's my card; call me anytime."

A moment later, the blue flashing lights pulsating through our living room disappeared, and he was gone.

Greg took a few minutes to pick up the bricks, future pavers for our back patio, and place them inside the back fence. Then he went to work on the pane. A lifetime before, he'd worked for a window manufacturer, repairing and reglazing windows. In less than fifteen minutes, the broken pane was as good as new, taken from a spare window he had saved. It looked untouched.

While he took care of that, I made coffee for both of us. We sat in our chairs, warming by the gas stove, trying to settle our rattled nerves.

I asked, "Do you think the brick is a message that we don't belong here? Everyone has been so good to us, but it makes me wonder."

Greg rubbed his forehead, every crease showing his exhaustion. "I think it's some teenager put up to a dare. The police officer thought so too." He drained his mug. "It's over and done. I'm tired. Let's try to get some sleep if we can." Suddenly, he grinned. "One funny thing is if they come back, they can't even show their buddies what they did."

Returning our mugs to the sink, I chuckled to think of the vandals returning to see their handiwork, but the glass now looking as if it never happened. Where is the fun in vandalizing if you can't show it to your friends?

"I didn't want to give them the satisfaction of knowing they got one over on us," Greg said as we trudged toward the bedroom.

I pulled down the comforter and slid in next to him, my hero.

This disruption wasn't going to complicate things. Greg and I were going to finish this restoration if it killed us. But after that night, we began to wonder if it might.

Chapter 2

WE FOUND OUR COTTAGE

*M*Y CRAFTSMAN HUSBAND, GREG, WORKED for Liollio Architecture, a firm that had spent more than sixty years designing in Charleston. He was very aware of what a typical renovation in this town would require of us. Each house was like opening a time capsule with hopes of discovering buried treasure. Each phase of the process came under scrutiny to ensure the house preserved its southern heritage.

Despite the constraints, however, Greg and I shared a dream of owning a house on the Charleston peninsula. In 2012, we decided to pursue that dream. We had looked at the surrounding suburbs but were drawn to live in this exciting city. Upscale neighborhoods, old-world charm, the convenience of walking to all the local restaurants—this was where we wanted to be.

We enlisted real estate agent Leon Polk to help us find a small cottage to restore on the upper West Side. Several weeks passed, and several opportunities collapsed due to quick sales or poor timing. Taking matters into our own hands, Greg and I spent evenings religiously surfing realty sites and tax maps looking for the right place.

Leon was happy to let us search because he believed we were looking for a pipe dream, something impossible to find. What we appreciated most about him was his willingness to show us anything, anywhere. Greg was faithful to do searches for many weeks.

We found several deplorable houses, so bad no one dared tackle them. Despite neighborhoods that didn't appear safe, many prices remained out of our reach. Carefully vetting each place, we settled on three potential houses within a few blocks of each other.

On a clear morning in late fall 2011, we set out with Leon to take a look. The first house on the list was halfway down a quiet, dead-end street. Leon pointed out several newly remodeled homes that would add to our value from day one. He quickly spieled off the selling points. As we listened, we noticed a large, vacant lot next to the home. Although the space might seem an advantage at first, it meant a house could be built within an arm's length of us.

Inside, Greg discovered that vandals had ripped out all the copper pipes. The floor levels varied from room to room. With practiced ease, Greg tallied up the cost and the work. Something about the house did not feel right with either of us.

We asked to move on to the others on the list. Leon kept going on about this being a far safer place to live than the others on the list, but we weren't convinced.

We wanted that special feeling from the spirit of the house but hadn't found it yet.

The second house was a Charleston Cottage built in the late 1920s. Our first impression was a front courtyard surrounded by a classic Charleston wrought iron fence. Its heavy, pointed spires had all the craftmanship found in better parts of the city. Although the fence remained strong, the tiny garden inside was neglected, filled with a hideous overgrown tree and a mound of debris. Paint chips from the peeling porch flecked the ground. The rusty gate's closure had long since vanished, leaving it to blow willy-nilly in the breeze, squeaking every time it moved.

Sagging and broken down, a haphazard addition hung on the side of the structure with barely enough height to stand upright. A strange looking block wall stood next to the street.

The interior was a hoarder's nest piled so full we could barely see the condition of the structure. The original two rooms looked to be in the best condition apart from their tilting floors. We smelled mildew and looked up to see a leaky roof.

The current occupant had rented in these conditions for more than twenty years. After the house was sold, they would move to city housing. The lady of the house told us that leaving their home grieved them. However, I knew Charleston city housing offered more safety and comfort, as well as rent based on their income.

Needless to say, the neighborhood was sketchy. Street signs denoted, "No selling or handling of drugs allowed." The lampposts held more than one wanted poster.

The house was the eyesore of this seasoned community and had been on the market for more than a year. Later, Greg learned the Charleston Cottage was on the condemned list if no one rescued it. In a city that resisted tearing anything down, that news validated its dire state.

A friend of ours lived nearby. She informed us that the cross street intersecting a few hundred feet from our door was known for late night deals and unpredicted violence. Though the houses on Congress Street were in bad shape, a few of the homes on the next street over, Race Street, were already renovated. The area had great potential to come back.

Already fatigued with looking, we still had one more house to evaluate. We drove to Line Street down by the bay area. Immediately, the neighborhood appeared less than desirable. Groups of young men lined the sidewalks.

"Greg!" I gasped when a small teen wearing a 3X T-shirt knocked on Greg's window. When he opened the window about two inches, the kid said, "You'll have to come back because the po-po are still parked at the church."

Greg looked a little shocked and waved in acknowledgment, trying to get out of the situation any way he could. We kept right on driving, and none of us breathed until we were three blocks away. When we stopped at a red light, and Greg started chuckling, I giggled. He put his hand over mine, and we laughed until the light turned green.

Finally, I managed to say, "Your first drug deal, and you didn't even score." More laughing, but it wasn't really funny. What were we thinking?

Still, we couldn't quit.

As we sat in Leon's office for a debriefing of the day, he said, "Are you sure you want to do this? I have real concerns. I have to warn you, the first house is in the safest location, and I wouldn't live there myself. I cannot see how you would even consider the other two. So I am showing you them with the disclaimer *buy at your own risk*. Got it? If you find more to look at, please let me know. Thank God you didn't force me out on Line Street."

We knew he was right to be concerned, but we were not looking for the typical purchase. Over the next few weeks, we continued to explore. We had to do more research about the area and the direction of the city.

Oddly enough, during this time a policeman stopped me on a routine traffic stop, and I took the chance to ask his opinion about the upper West Side.

"We are considering buying a house there. Is it a safe enough neighborhood?"

CONSTRUCTION BREAK
Connecting

From the earliest days of marriage, making a fresh start requires effort and concession—a willingness to embrace change. Often it comes with the struggle of making life work but also with a promise of home: a place to rest, to be who we are, to feel truly loved and accepted. Often, opening up our mess means adjusting to our anxieties, habits, and struggles, which can be worse than we anticipate. We must keep our eyes on the goal to connect.

"Crime still finds its way to that area though it is less and less," he said. "It can be an occasional gunshot, a home burglary, or a car stolen, but if you endure through this transition period, you'll have a prime piece of Charleston real estate." His words gave me hope that living in the Charleston Cottage might just work for us.

An architect from Greg's firm owned a house a block away from the Charleston Cottage. She and her family had purchased their house two years prior. She assured us that while Senate Street was the most dangerous street near us, she saw the promise of Congress Street. Purchasing while costs are low meant living in less-secure conditions until the tide turned. We had to decide what we were willing to live with in the short term. The Charleston Cottage's purchase price was less than the value of the property it rested upon, and that kept us interested.

We called Leon and met him for a second look at the cottage. After another walk-through, Greg and I took a few moments to stand on the sidewalk across the street from its iron gate.

"What do you think, Denise?" he asked me.

"It is by far the roughest house we've done, Greg, but there is something about it I'm drawn to. I can't explain it. Everyone's going to think we have lost our minds. Literally. I think it's the gate and the beautiful spires surrounding the courtyard that draws me. An artisan who made wrought iron for the wealthy invested in his art here."

"I feel the very same way," he replied. "There is nothing logical about buying such a broken heap in this neighborhood. We don't know what we are facing once we open it up, yet there is a hidden treasure here." Greg grabbed my hand. "If you're with me, Denise, I can promise you there is nothing in this mess we cannot fix."

That moment the decision formed in our hearts. We still weighed the choice long and hard, but none of the red flags dissuaded us.

This wasn't love at first sight, but we knew it was something special. This was a personal investment that went beyond the dollars in the purchase price. The Charleston Cottage had good bones with life left in them.

Several weeks later, we closed on the cottage, purchasing the property for little more than the price of a new car. As we sat across from our attorney at closing, an elderly African American

CONSTRUCTION BREAK
Marriage Holes

All marriages have holes. That's a given. The holes are places where we disconnect: containers for selfishness, for disappointment, and for addictions as we try to find alternatives for unmet needs. If you wonder why you fight most with those you love best, intimacy exposes our underbelly of shame and guilt. Intimacy opens up the holes. Growing means making small movements toward each other, coming together to reduce friction. People tend to view each other's faults as the source of their stress, but all we can control is our own attitude and response. When we choose to understand our spouse, we can reduce immediate frustration and open ourselves to connection. Extend grace and take time to look deeper. By considering the other person's deeper needs, we earn the right to speak the truth of our own needs.

woman with a walker shuffled into the room with her daughter. She was the only surviving member of the Moultrie family who had owned the house since 1940. Born in Charleston, she left at age eighteen to live in Philadelphia for the remainder of her life. Her brother, Eugene, inherited the house from her father, and it became a rental. Many local families raised their children in this house. At Eugene's death, the house had passed to her.

After the papers were signed, she said, "I grew up in this house, and I have many good memories there, but it is time to move on. I have to depend on others to take care of the rental issues, which, as you can see, are mounting." She smiled. "Can you jack it up and make it a two story, Mr. Broadwater?"

Greg replied, "We have to come up with a plan, but most likely we will keep it a small Charleston single house with a side piazza. I promise to respectfully restore it back to better than original. We hope you will follow our blog and remain in touch with us, ma'am."

"I don't do the computer, but my granddaughter is up on all that stuff," she said. "I couldn't be happier you are saving it."

And so, the longer-than-expected journey began.

What about You?

- Greg and Denise acted as a team and consulted each other about deciding on what home to purchase. Do you feel your spouse considers you in major decisions? What if there is an impasse? Does your opinion count?

- They were influenced by all they had experienced in the past. Their experiences made them consider different aspects as they searched for a house. Has your past drawn you together as you consider the future, or has it driven a wedge between you?

- Like this older cottage, do you believe there is nothing in your marriage that cannot be fixed if you are both willing to sacrifice to make it happen?

Chapter 3

LOVE ALMOST AT FIRST SIGHT

"*I*'M SORRY, SIR." THE YOUNG valet at the Boat-house on Isle of Palms shook his head. "I cannot park your car if you're not on our register."

Greg's cheeks turned pink, and perspiration beaded on his forehead. "Didn't you make a reservation, Denise?" His tone showed his disappointment in my failure.

Our church's small group had plans to enjoy a final night of food and fellowship before we disbanded for the summer. Now this.

"I called twice, Greg. I promise. Someone dropped the ball." I was already scrambling to find another place. As soon as I began texting another couple from our group, the phone buzzed.

It was Julia saying, "Denise, I hope it's OK with you, but Dean and I are holding a table at Sol."

Sol was just a few minutes away. "Julia, what a relief! Thanks for finding a space to fit all of us."

We headed to Sol, and Greg's stress faded once all eight of us were conversing over our menus.

Julia's husband, Dean, sat next to Greg and launched into a conversation. "How would you like to go on a fishing trip, Greg?"

Greg perked up. He loved to fish. As Dean continued the sales pitch, I saw a glimmer arise in Greg's eyes. Once again, our house renovation stood in the way of an opportunity to have fun.

Dean pushed ahead. "Greg, we are talking about half the month of June in a pristine, Canadian preserve, and we will be on the only private property in miles and miles of wilderness. The northern lights and beauty alone are worth the trip. Add to it catching your limit of walleye, pike, and small mouth every day." He leaned forward. "Come on, man. You know you want to go. Y'all can have a big fish fry with your take of the catch."

He turned his attention to me. "Maybe you'll invite Denise if she's good enough to letcha go." He was playing hardball, staring at me with an intentional grin.

Dean's friendship with Greg grew out Greg's transparency in our church marriage group about his own struggles with me. Since early in our meetings, I suspected Dean was eyeing Greg for induction to man-cave-dweller status. Dean was faithful to our Sunday night meetings. I was naïve enough to think my charm and witty leadership methods kept Dean in that chair discussing his issues.

Then I realized it had nothing to do with me.

"Denise, are your reins too tight on our poor Greg?" Dean said. "Where is the individual balance in that? You've been saying all the right things in small group, but here is the opportunity to live out what ya been saying."

Dean was using my own Venn diagram against me. I could have reacted in one of two ways—express with words the heat rising up my neck or consider the possibility this man might be right. As much as I hated to admit it, Greg needed time for himself. Dean's eyes were fixed on me, but all I could see was his outstretched arm dangling a Canadian fishing trip in front of Greg's overworked eyes.

"Dean McMahon, you are putting on the charm tonight," I said.

We both leaned back and chuckled. He knew Greg and I were headlong into the plight of weekend projects. However, his words caused me to question how much I allowed Greg the freedom to get away for some man-time.

As dinner ended, Dean stepped aside to whisper to me as I gathered my things, "Denise, you need to make this happen. Greg needs to take me up on this. It's a chance of a lifetime for

CONSTRUCTION BREAK

Free to be Me

Although the Bible says we "become one flesh" speaking of the sexual union, we are not to lose ourselves when we marry. We come into the relationship with individual needs, likes, and ideas. Maintaining personal friendships, developing professionally, engaging in hobbies, and recharging our inner lives through retreat are all examples of maintaining spiritual and mental health. The marriage relationship has a better chance of survival when two healthy individuals come together to connect. To restrict or place counterproductive demands on our spouses is to suffocate and hurt potential intimacy growth.

someone who enjoys fishing. We both know he needs this."

All I could do was smile knowingly at Dean because at that moment, I knew Greg was going to Canada. Taking a trip was nothing short of irresponsible. Room after room was now demo-ed down to the frame. We lived in constant disarray, and now our project would be derailed, *again*.

I sighed. Life went on regardless. If we were to be balanced, we needed to allow detours for the sake of our marriage and for sheer sanity. I knew that, but about day three alone in the house, I also knew I would regret this.

I said, "Dean, thanks for giving him this opportunity. He is going to love it."

Dean left the restaurant with a spring in his step and the smile of a winner.

Driving home, Greg and I were both quiet. Finally, I broke the ice. "Greg, I want you to work out the details and go on this trip." The words dropped from my lips, and I heard them with my ears but couldn't believe I was saying them.

Since living on Congress Street, I'd never stayed in the Charleston house solo, and the thought gave me a feeling of dread. Things came up at the house when you least expected them, such as the inner-city-crime thing, and the air-conditioner-breaker thing, and the outside-security thing. You get my drift? How could I encourage Greg to go to Canada for two weeks? Did I fail to mention our thirty-year-anniversary thing happening days before he was scheduled to leave? This would even mean postponing any kind of trip to celebrate as a couple. What's more, I didn't think in our thirty years together we had ever spent eighteen nights away from one another; there had been nothing more than a week-long work trip or extended weekend.

Greg glanced my way. "It would use up all but a week of my vacation time, Denise. I am not sure committing so much time to something unproductive is the right thing to do . . . although it does sound pretty fantastic." Greg knew the sacrifice I would be making because our time off for the rest of the year would be limited. However, the guilt didn't last long when he got to thinking of a clear, untainted lake full of large fish in the Ontario wilderness.

"You need this, Greg," I told him. "You need to get off the grid and not have to think. Unwind from all your projects, from our Charleston Cottage, and maybe even from me." I threw myself in the mix to get a rise out of him.

He put his hand on my arm and shook me. We both laughed. We were bonded to each other like two pieces of glued wood, but we could use a healthy dose of separation from time to time.

I said, "Talk to your boss and see what he can do to make it happen." Greg's boss depended on him as much as I did.

"I will ask him if he can live without me for two weeks, but I am not going to get my hopes too high."

The next day, I got Greg's text: "I am off, Denise. The boss is making it happen. Looks like I am headed to Ontario for the better part of June! Can you handle staying on Congress Street? Are you sure you want me to do this?"

With all the bravery I could muster, I texted back, "Sure. It's time I grow up, don't ya think?" My brow tensed at the very thought of managing on my own in this inner-city neighborhood and his leaving in less than two weeks. I knew that without him I could never navigate living here with my anxieties. Most of the newbies to these streets usually had a rather large dog on a leash and, after our experiences, I understood their reasoning.

This extended time of separation brought up a surge of memories about my uncertainty at the beginning of our relationship.

～

I had been date-free through six years of college. If I blossomed before graduation, I couldn't have told you, but something changed. Perhaps my complexion had cleared. Perhaps I found a hairstyle that wrestled my unruly locks into something flattering. Perhaps I became more fit.

Back then, I blamed my outward appearance for my dating desert. It might have been my lack of confidence, my tendencies to be opinionated and serious-minded, or my plain pigheadedness. But, for some reason, by the end of grad school, suitors started popping up all over the place. They put out feelers about my status; they talked to my friends about who I might be dating and whether I would consider going out, attempting to avoid a turn down. Some did the noble thing and approached me directly. It mattered little because I refused all offers. To be honest, I was angry. These men had been around me for years. Month after month without a date, I'd attended functions with my girlfriends, and the feeling of rejection left an indelible mark on my self-esteem. I didn't trust this surge of male interest to be genuine.

My good friend, Ron, from undergrad days hung out in the campus coffee shop most afternoons, and I was anxious to find a sympathetic ear. As I entered the student center, I was relieved to see him at his usual table, his tall and lanky form bent over a book.

I dropped my books onto the table. "Ron, I hate to bother you, but I am in way over my head."

Ron looked up and smiled, laying down his pencil. Apart from my best friend, Melanie, I couldn't think of anyone else I would rather confide in. Ron knew me best.

"Who, Denise? The strongest woman I know?"

"Hey, listen up. I've had three guys ask me out in the past week, and I am having all these emotions. I'm mad, sad, afraid to leave my room, afraid another guy will approach me. Is desperation written all over me?"

"Isn't this what you've been waiting for, Denise?"

I laid my cheek down on the cool table, exasperated. "I'm scared! I date at home in the summers, but then I have an escape route when I come back to college. These guys look much more permanent."

Ron said, "It's not like these guys are random strangers. A date is not an engagement. Maybe this surge is their graduation jitters about leaving school without a potential wife." He frowned. "God, I hope not!"

I sat up and looked at Ron. *Surely not!*

Ron tilted his head, and his dark hair flopped onto his forehead. With great nonchalance he said, "I am hoping you might consider dating Greg from our singles group. If you ever started dating, you two'd be married before the end of the year."

"You must have me confused with someone else," I told him. "Go tell your friend, Greg, he'll have to get in line."

"*He* never mentions you to me. The guy's too shy to let me know if he's got his eye on you. I've had this reoccurring thought about the two of you for a while now. Trust me, Denise, I've got good instincts."

Ron was right on that count. He seemed to have an uncanny ability to predict things. I made a mental note to check Greg out next time we were at Sunday school, but played it down with, "Well, let's not put too much into your intuitive skills on matters of *my* heart."

Ron frowned. "I am a bit shocked you are taking this so hard, Denise. You have tons of guy friends. You major in theology, a field dominated by men, and if I remember right, over half of them come to you for dating advice, right?"

"Yeah, I can advise, but this is a whole 'nother thing."

Maybe it was my wicked stepfather stigma that put me off with guys. He had seemed so perfect to my mom early on, but within two months of their wedding, we found out he was different than he had made himself out to be. We all suffered. I couldn't afford to make the same mistake, so a man had to be pretty special for me to take the leap.

I grabbed my books. "Ron, I can count on you to set me straight. You get back to studying." Walking toward the door, I felt shaky inside. My inner wounds ran deeper than anyone would suspect, even me. I wanted a serious relationship, but I needed to be sure. Unfortunately, being completely sure didn't exist.

After church the following week, a slender middle-aged woman approached me as I gathered my things.

"Denise, do you know who I am?"

"No, ma'am, I don't."

"I am Sarah Broadwater."

"Hi. How are you? I've heard your name; are your sons in our singles group?"

"Yes, they are. When I heard there is a Mast in their Sunday school class, I thought you might be an Amish girl."

"My parents were born Amish but left the church when they were young. The Mast name is as Amish as they come."

"Are you from Ohio?" Sarah persisted.

"Can you believe Dover, Delaware? Dover is primarily an Ohio Amish settlement. My parents became Conservative Mennonite before they were married. Why do you ask?"

"I'm from the Amish in Hartville, Ohio. Why don't you come over sometime and have dinner at my house, and we can talk more?"

I would've never guessed the Broadwater men were related to the Amish. By midweek, Sarah arranged a dinnertime for me to visit. They lived in a modest ranch-style house. When I arrived, four of Sarah's sons were seated around the table. Greg (Ron's pick) had medium brown hair and brown eyes. Thin and wiry, his hands were calloused from hard work.

Everyone was very quiet. If this Greg was destined to be my future husband, he'd have to exert himself a bit more.

Dinner conversation with Sarah was welcoming, and I was thankful for a homecooked meal after months of dining on common food.

After dinner, Sarah and I retired to the living room sofa, and she pulled out her Amish genealogies. We saw no immediate shared relatives except for Sarah's cousin, Magdalena, who married one in my mother's family.

Months passed after the Broadwater dinner. In April, I was hanging out with Ron again when he asked, "Are you going to Debbie and Tom's wedding next week?"

"Yeah, I am going with Melissa. Feel free to join us, Ron. Melissa won't care. I don't know the couple well outside of singles group, so I'd prefer going with a few friends."

"Sorry, I can't come. I am going up to visit my mom that weekend. I am thinking of looking for a job in New York and returning home this fall."

"Ron, I'll miss you!" I laughed. "So, I won't have you to protect me at the reception? We could give people something to talk about."

"You are on your own there. Stop worrying and have fun!"

At the reception, I took my typical wallflower position, observing everyone else. I needed to warm up and get my bearings in these types of social settings. I spied Greg sitting across the room in a chair against the opposite wall. He looked good in his suit, though I preferred darker brown hair. Something about him appealed to me, but he was so darn quiet. Such a quiet guy was not part of my ideal man, and I was not sure how that would work out.

He said hi to me when I passed him on my way in; at least that was something.

Melissa was with me when Greg made his way over to us. When he placed himself next to me, she conveniently decided to refresh her drink.

Here we go, I said to myself.

Greg relaxed against the wall and nervously chit-chatted about singles group. Both of us felt awkward. *God help us.*

And then the words fell out.

"Denise, would you go to a dinner with me this coming Friday night? Every few months my former employer asks my brothers and me to find dates every few months, and we go out for steaks at the Angus Steak House on Cervantes. I think it would be fun."

"I like a good steak. Sure."

"What staff housing are you in over at the college?"

"Griffith."

"Pick you up around 6:00 p.m.?"

"Thanks for including me. Sounds like fun." I was

saying the words, but inside I was unsure. When he walked away, I was so glad that exchange was over. I was amazed he got the words out. I thought I might have to help him. When Ron heard about this, he was going to have a heyday. But he could not be right about the rest of his prediction.

On Monday night, Ron moseyed into our study area in the coffee shop and sat at my table.

"Ron, something happened while you were at your mom's this weekend."

"Sounds serious. What?"

"Greg Broadwater asked me out, and I agreed."

"You are going out with Greg?" He let out a hoot. "What did I tell you?"

"It's a date, Ron, not an engagement."

"I'll be getting an invitation one of these days . . . wait and see." We laughed as good friends do, and I knew I deserved his bit of teasing. I couldn't help but wonder about his prediction.

Greg picked me up in a new Ford truck, and our first drive together went smoothly. I could tell he was making an effort to ask me questions and be interested.

"Chucky Tanger owns a local furniture store. It's his retirement store. Just know, he's a big tease, and I am afraid you are on the hot seat being a new kid on the block." Greg looked at me sideways, watching for my reaction. He fidgeted with his leather watchband.

"Chucky hires us to do deliveries and move his inventory in the store," he went on.

"That's its own type of job security right there. If

you're a Broadwater, you have a job at Tangers. Good deal." I avoided the hot-seat comment. I could handle whatever came my way. As we rode, I opened my purse, checked my lipstick, and popped in a breath mint.

"Doug and Suzanne, my older brother and his wife, will be at dinner with us."

When we arrived, Chucky came out to meet us. He had gray hair with a bald patch on top; he was a man who looked every bit of seventy. He reached to shake my hand and held it for an extended period of time. My face turned red, and I could tell he was teasing Greg.

Watching them interact, it was obvious Chucky loved these boys like sons. During dinner, the sarcasm and teasing continued. Chucky told me he tested all the boys' dates to see if they could handle the Broadwater wit. I fired back at Chucky, and he liked my spunk.

A true gentleman, Greg dropped me off with no attempt to kiss me at the door. It was easy and comfortable.

Greg's patience with me was the foundation of our love, and it continues to this day. My trust in him

CONSTRUCTION BREAK
Mutual Respect

A profound sense of respect is part of the foundation laid in the early months of a relationship. Beyond any initial attraction, it is the glue that holds the relationship together. Knowing my spouse has my best interest at heart no matter the external circumstances, is key to a growing relationship. If there are signs of contempt early on, the probability of surviving drops regardless of the connectedness. Contempt is disdain at the core and comes out in little ways, chipping away at the marriage foundation.

developed over time. Greg was my first experience of unconditional love after a dysfunctional mess in my family. Day by day, our love grew.

My mother's choices around my stepfather, Elliott, were part of my developmental fabric. Independent minded and entrepreneurial prior to dating him, my mother was still fooled, and her misjudgment cost us all. My take on her situation is that she should have waited so his true colors could emerge. Waiting would have spared us the hurt we suffered at Elliott's hand.

So then I was faced with my own leap of faith. My fear about making the same mistake plagued me.

Greg pursued me despite my reservations, and Ron's prediction came true. Our first date, May 2, led to a wedding date on May 23 the following year.

Thirty plus years later, I have no regrets. How thankful I am I took a leap of faith in trusting Greg with my heart, my life, and my future. We have holes and struggles, but Greg remains God's shining light to me. If we gained this house and lost our love, we would have lost everything. If we lost this house and failed in this venture, yet emerged with our love intact, we would be most blessed. Like any long-term marriage, we fight our battles but continue to win the war. Underneath all of it, I attribute my successes and opportunities to Greg. His life is a God-light filling my emotional deficits with sound reason. I am so grateful for how he weathers life, and now this house, with me. He refuses to give up.

I would miss him these weeks in Canada, but I

knew he would come back to me refreshed and ready to battle this renovation journey once more.

What about You?

- How secure was your foundation of trust when you were dating? How does Greg and Denise's story differ from yours?

- Did you develop respect for each other? Why or why not?

- Have the years since your marriage taken their toll on the mutual respect you began with? Or has that deepened with time?

- If it is less, is there hope for the respect to be restored?

Chapter 4

Dragged through the Mud

A construction professional, Greg oddly didn't give me, his teammate, any clue about his projected completion date. When I brought up timing in passing conversation, he was noncommittal. I was torn without a long-term plan. He obviously didn't want the confines of a deadline. After living through a new-build project more than twenty years prior, I knew his attention to detail and the perfectionism that pervades all parts of his work.

He wanted to be hands on in every aspect of this project. He had no intention of hiring subcontractors. The benefit was quality workmanship, but the downside was months and months of camp-style living in an unfinished house.

Although we felt optimistic and happy for several months, eventually reality hit.

When Greg got home one evening, I said, "The bathroom creeps me out. The hair stands up on the back of my neck when I walk through that room. It's almost like a presence. I don't believe in lost roaming souls, but I can't seem to get past it."

Greg chuckled. "Maybe you've been on one too many ghost walks on the Battery." When he noticed my nonsmiling face, his expression tensed. "I am fighting a leaning foundation and a crawlspace full of trash. Once I am done with the structural repairs, we can frame the new bath." He hugged me. "Hang in there. We're still a few months out."

A few days later, he pulled up some floorboards in the kitchen, and an awful smell drove me out to the piazza. I yelled through the open door, "What is it? Smells like something's dead."

From inside, I heard Greg's muffled voice. "Looks like the kitchen sink drain was running out onto the ground under the house. I'll have to spread lime to clean up the bacteria." He came to the doorway. "It may take a few days to break down the odor. I haven't seen this level of code violation in years."

I fought the urge to gag. "Gross."

The problem was more severe than Greg predicted. He ended up knee deep in the muck, shoveling out putrid soil day after day, hauling it out in buckets. I must have gone olfactory blind during those days. Even now, I don't know how I got through it.

Eventually, only clean dry dirt remained, but it was still open dirt in the kitchen.

After weeks of this, I was beyond belief. Holding a broom in my hands, I walked to the door that looked into the abyss of the open floor system and dirt, lots of dirt, and I leaned against the door jam. Greg was clearing out the last remaining debris prior to framing the floor system. I sighed.

"What is it, Denise?" His voice sounded edgy. "I can tell you are frustrated."

"Couldn't we find a framer to get this floor system done this week? Then we could move on to the bathroom."

"We can't afford to hire it out, and I hope to have it started this weekend. I'd probably end up reworking what they do anyway."

I shifted against the door with a rising feeling inside my throat. I was whining, but I needed to vent. The mess was getting to me.

Greg stood up straight and stared at me. "Why are you pushing me, Denise? You remember agreeing to support me? I cannot help that the foundation was so much worse than we thought. You've done this kind of work with me before, so you knew some of what we are facing here."

I stared back at him. "Nothing we have done in the past has involved living with an open floor for months. I am about to lose it."

"I am doing all I can do." Greg stabbed at the dirt with his rake and leaned into the job.

Saying more was not going to make a difference. I trudged into our efficiency apartment in the front room. Dropping the broom, I plopped down on the bed and let the tears flow.

Who else would live in such conditions? At this rate, we would be stuck with this lifestyle for several more years. How much more could I take? All I wanted was a covered floor, a clean bathroom, and a kitchen with a stove and a sink.

Beyond that, I wanted to be OK, to be at ease. I wanted to not dread washing my dishes in a plastic laundry sink or washing myself in that gross bathroom.

Worse, multiple times per day I came face to face with my imagination of what might be slithering or slinking through those holes. I was grateful my clients couldn't witness their therapist tiptoeing in plastic flip-flops, knees high, prancing through that area, hypervigilant as I washed dishes, showered in the rusty bathtub, or tinkled in the leaky toilet.

Greg's logical words cycled through my brain: "You need to get over this. I crawl under this house on a weekly basis, and nothing is there." But his words didn't help. I had to face my demons on my own.

I resented that Greg had no anxiety, and I was a wreck. It was all too easy for him. His logical mind couldn't understand my terror, and that hurt the most.

I sat up and raised the blind

CONSTRUCTION BREAK
Recovery Is Key

When there is conflict or intense response, step away to bring down the emotion before any more damage is done to the relationship. During this cooling-off period, we must consider our own attitudes and tones in communicating. (We can only change ourselves.) Come back together with the purpose of resolving it. Share our needs with each other. Be understanding and offer validation. Keep in mind, we want to be closer than we were before the fight. This cycle repeats, especially when at an impasse. A poor job of managing recovery hurts bring further disconnection and eats away at our foundations. At times, we have to allow each other our differing positions and move toward tolerance.

to see a group of young men across the street. The rhythmic boom of a subwoofer came from a car that slowed to talk to them. Litter blew down the street. Children played basketball using a sidewalk hoop. This was our new neighborhood.

How could Greg ask me why I didn't see this coming? I felt like I was tricked.

On the other hand, we couldn't quit now. We had to see it through.

Like a broken record, Greg's recurring words were, "I am doing all I can to get us comfortable again, but we have to live through this part." Every few months, we had this same heated discussion. I didn't want it to chip away at the foundation of our marriage.

Some of my mood might have been related to our closing on the sale of our former family home to help finance this renovation. I cried when we handed over the keys to another family. Until then, we would sometimes steal away from Charleston for a restful weekend at our old home on the lake and catching up with friends. That chapter of our life was closed. Now the Charleston Cottage was our only place, our new home.

This day, I hated that the structure was torn open from stem to stern, opened to the elements and whatever vermin wandered through. Somehow I needed to come to terms with it.

I laid on the bed, wiping my damp face. All this worry didn't change anything, but how could I pull myself together?

When friends and coworkers visited us, they

would watch Greg on the jobsite and enjoy the show. They said to me, "Who can do all this anymore?"

I nodded and smiled.

Greg's gift was a rare find. His training came from a day when pride in workmanship took priority over a quick finish. Building was in his bones; like his father and grandfather before him, Greg had an unmistakable talent. For him, craftsmanship was therapy. For me, it was something far different. While I burst with pride over Greg's skill, it did nothing to reduce my suffering through daily life.

The house's holes would forever remain etched into my memory. The holes migrated to new locations with each new project; they were relentless. They cried out to me.

My soul was weary as I sat on my bed with a window air conditioner continually blowing and an overhead fan whirring to keep us cool during the dog days of summer in Charleston. I longed for quiet. Sometimes I wondered if we were starting to forget what it meant to live with basic comforts.

Through all this, we still strived to find life balance such as maintaining important relationships, seeing our young-adult children and aging parents, and finding time for each other.

Our lives were made up of much more than a house, and I didn't want anything in our world to become a casualty of Greg's need for quality workmanship.

A few months passed, and the weeks ran together. One afternoon the sun beat hard onto my back as I stepped from my car and opened the hatch to pick up a few bags of essentials purchased on my way home. My computer bag swung from one arm leaving my hands free for the groceries. All I wanted to do was to get things put away, so I could rest my head for a few minutes. Decompressing from hours of active listening at the office was part of my daily self-care.

Like punching a time clock, a small crowd of men arrived each morning to sit on the front porch directly across the street from our piazza door. Their daily gathering brought a stream of steady traffic. Although naïve to their world, I knew why they were here. The boom boxes and dark-windowed, sleek vehicles gave a clue to their secret business.

I felt their eyes on me as I gathered my packages.

Sonny, the apparent head man, walked toward me. "Hey, miss, how you doin'?"

My heart thumped, but I kept my voice light. "Hey, it's hot out here. I don't know how you guys stand it." Over his shoulder, I spotted a city sign warning that distribution of illegal substances was a crime, and this area was monitored.

"The shade of the porch helps," he said. "Let Greg know your waterline sprung a leak this afternoon. If you look down Carondolet, you'll see the spray of water onto the street. I didn't have any way to reach him, or I'd have called to help with that leak and water bill." He smiled, friendly and casual. "Need any help carryin' those bags?"

My forehead beaded up with perspiration. "Sonny, I appreciate your offer, but it's one trip. Y'all watch out for our place, and we appreciate it. I'll call Greg and get the water shut off." I closed the hatch. "Things are so old and fragile here; it's bound to happen until we get stuff changed over." Smiling, I said, "Listen, stay cool. Thanks for reaching out."

"You too. Greg's doing a great job."

A neighbor said that Sonny had been a talented chef in one of the downtown restaurants, but this new money came easier. I raised my hand in a brief wave to the other men as Sonny moved back to his porch. Others had lived here for years and were fine. I tried to keep that in mind. After all, it was much too hot to get worked up over stuff when I had to figure out how I was going to get through the evening without water.

Inside, I deposited my heavy computer bag and grocery sacks on the makeshift counter. Someone else might not have called this a kitchen. A utility table with a hot plate and microwave stood to one side, our dorm-sized refrigerator was beneath the table to avoid wasting floor space. A rolling cart under the table held my pots and pans.

As I started dinner, I recalled the first day we set up this room. We pulled up the worn-through carpet then swept and mopped this floor. Our excitement fueled our demolition. We overlooked the worn sheetrock, the bare lightbulb overhead, and the peeling paint. We were proud owners of a small plot of Charleston history, and our minds could only think about wonderful possibilities.

After wiping down the walls, Greg sprayed a thin paint boundary between us and the grimy decayed shell. The parched walls of that room drank in five gallons of paint. Once the paint dried, we spread a large carpet. An Asian-style full-sized bed filled one side of the room and a leather sectional the other. Our coffee table became storage, tabletop, and footrest. Greg screwed the TV base to the leaning fireplace mantel. He installed a closet wire shelf in an alcove next to the fireplace with a thrift-store dresser underneath and storage boxes on top.

That night we unrolled our house plans across our bed and dreamed.

Greg and I pulled together those first months in that front room. We waited on approval of our plans and our permit. Greg began the demolition. Teamwork brought us renewed love for each other, a surge of passion that was surprising after several decades of being together.

We were happy for many reasons. I had the opportunity to go minimal and establish a new routine. Greg got to work with his hands after several years at a desk. Drawing on our inner strengths and our common resolve, we were able to sustain for several months.

Unfortunately, those blissful days were long gone.

I closed my eyes and heard the *boom, boom, boom* of another car pulling up. I asked God if he would please bring me some peace and quiet, so I could recharge after a long day with clients. Emotionally spent, I drifted off to sleep.

A few nights later, I arrived home after work, and Sonny ran over to me. "Guess what?" he said. "My aunt's house is sold. We couldn't believe it happened so fast."

"Sonny, truly? Sold? That's quick." I saw his disappointment and understood that life was changing for all of us.

"She has been in a nursing home for at least two years, and I have been allowed on her porch, but the real estate agent came yesterday and told me I could not be here anymore. The new owner is renovating soon, and we don't have permission to stay." He stuck his hands in his pockets and looked off into our courtyard, a man in his mid-thirties, well built, and in his prime. He was overcome with sadness.

I said, "The neighborhood is being sold off one by one, isn't it? I am sure it is hard to see it go."

He managed a smile. "It sure is, but I like that the houses are getting fixed up. One of my guys was raised in your house and loves that you're not tearing it down. His mother and grandmother rented here for nearly twenty years, so they consider it their family home."

He gazed down the row of parked cars lining the street. "I've lived on these streets since I was a boy."

I smiled and shook my head with genuine sympathy. We paused for a long moment.

Finally, I moved. "Thanks for stopping by, Sonny. Please keep in touch with us when you are up our way. Be safe out there." I threw in that last comment with a genuine concern for his well-being and entered the house with a sigh of relief.

Living there had changed me. A few years before this, if you had told me I would become friends with a local drug dealer, I would have declared you crazy. Now, I counted it one of the richest parts of my journey on the West Side. Those men protected their turf, not wanting heat in their own backyard. I sensed his loyalty toward us as a part of his street. Nothing had been lifted from our jobsite to date, and I cannot help but believe Sonny was partially responsible for that.

I pushed my gate open, and it squeaked my arrival. Despite the taunts and apprehensive feedback from friends, stepping out to live in the house while we renovate was crucial to joining our community. Showing that we were willing to walk alongside neighbors like Sonny was part of this journey.

What about You?

• It was obvious that Denise valued Greg's construction ability, but she spoke of a downside to his talent. What was the downside? Was she right? Would it bother you?

• Most positives in a person have a negative that goes along with it. Can you pinpoint this in your spouse? In you?

• Are you willing to admit to what your spouse deals with in you?

Chapter 5

Opened to the Elements

Our one-room wonder in the front of the house slowly expanded to the middle area. Once the floor system in the kitchen had subflooring, Greg hung a few sets of simple wooden shelves from his dad's shop. He created makeshift cabinets using a salvaged door as a countertop over doorless lower cabinets.

It wasn't attractive, but I was over the moon to have this crude space. I stapled a curtain around the lower counter to hide our wares and reduce dust. In the center of the counter, a large cutting board created a wipeable cooking space. A new stainless steel refrigerator gleamed in the corner, and a gas stove sat in front of the fireplace. I felt opulent living in two rooms.

I was preparing a special celebration dinner when my cell phone rang. I heard the excitement in Greg's voice.

"Denise, the owner of a 1950s ranch on James Island is selling 1,000 square feet of the original hardwood floors from their house. From the pictures, I can tell the wood runs are longer, and the wood is a close match to the floors in our original two rooms. I'll drive over at lunch and see if there are enough salvaged pieces to make it worth purchasing. It's a fraction of the price of reclaimed flooring."

"Wow, and just in time. If I can mop the floor to keep this God-awful dust down, I'll be good." With a lilt in my voice, I said, "I'm making dinner. See you soon." I happily laid down the phone. Wearing my comfy slippers and house pants, I examined our existing floors and envisioned another woman from almost a century ago, cooking in front of this fireplace with a cast-iron pot full of soup for her husband and little ones. Many feet had stood where I stood that afternoon.

The aroma of fennel and garlic from my *zuppa toscana* filled the room—comfort in a bowl on this cool evening. A loaf of garlic bread warmed in the oven for dipping into the creamy goodness. All I could think about was how Greg's face would light up when he came home with our flooring and dinner was ready on our new stove. My love for cooking was therapy for me, a nice complement to Greg's love of hands-on construction.

As I stood at the stove, I glimpsed movement out of the corner of my eye. I looked over my shoulder and saw the gray-brown bushy tail of a raccoon moving slowly through the plastic curtain into the construction area.

I shut off the stove, stuck the soup pot into the

warm oven, and slammed the door behind me as I fled into the front efficiency room. My first impulse was to fire off an angry text to Greg, but I knew I'd regret what I would write in my current emotional state.

Instead, I trembled on the bed with a blanket over me. The longer I waited, the more I felt sorry for myself. How much of this was I supposed to stand? Heavens, I could have been bitten and had to endure rabies shots.

In minutes, Greg pulled up with his truck full of used hardwood flooring, all filled with nails and in need of cleaning. I dashed to the window. He looked pleased as he parked the truck. I waited, ready to pounce the moment he stepped inside.

My voice sounded strident: "Greg, you worked so hard to get me a more workable kitchen, and I loved making dinner, but"—strident turned to shrill— "I saw a gray bushy tail moving through the plastic curtain. A raccoon was right behind me when I was at the stove!" I wrapped my arms around my middle and rocked a little.

He looked shocked. "You saw it right there?"

CONSTRUCTION BREAK
Regulating the Response

We cannot control our sudden response to triggers that evoke strong emotions. However, we are responsible for how we regulate what comes next. Due to various backgrounds and levels of resiliency, one size does not fit all in managing responses. We must learn what works to lower our adrenalin once it kicks in. Some suggestions include breathing slowly, splashing our faces with cold water, or stepping outside for a change of scenery. These can help calm us. Controlling our frustration is more important than being right or winning.

Pointing, he stared at the plastic curtain. "A raccoon in this part of the house? Are you sure?"

"I hid the soup and ran to our room. I peeked out, but he didn't come back."

I pulled the soup out of the oven and set it back on top of the stove. Stirring, I continued, my words growing louder with every breath. "All these months, I washed my dishes in a plastic laundry sink and showered in flip-flops, always wondering if I might fall through the dilapidated bathtub at any moment, but hear me, *I don't do animals in the house that can bite me in my sleep!*" I dropped the spoon against the side of the pot and faced him. "We may as well be homeless!"

Greg stood motionless with astonishment on his face. He heard the resolve in my voice. Slowly his astonishment faded to a humorous glint, but he didn't dare laugh in front of me.

A tinge of guilt crept into my heart as I already regretted the things I had said. After all, the raccoon was not Greg's fault. It was part of living in an open construction building. Constant stress was causing us both to fall back into arguing like we had earlier in our marriage. Though I was not prepared to admit it just yet, I knew he wasn't the only one who'd signed up for this.

However, all I could envision right then was an army of raccoons, feral cats, rats, and God knows what else attacking us as we sleep.

Greg scurried throughout that side of the house, covering the large holes in the floor by nailing boards and wood scraps over them and filling the smaller ones with pink insulation. Last, he nailed plywood over the plastic door where the raccoon had entered.

Later that night, I lay in bed, crying to release my raw emotions, wondering how I could continue there under those conditions. Greg came over and held me tight. This was the strength of our love without words.

One Sunday morning not long after our furry visitor, we reached home knowing that we needed this day to rest. We had a longstanding habit of eating a nice after-church dinner followed by an afternoon nap. As we pulled into our parking spot, Greg caught a glimpse of another kind of visitor through the wrought iron spires. A man lounged on our piazza just inside the courtyard.

Just as Greg pointed him out to me, the man slipped out the open gate and disappeared around the corner of the house. We imagined he was looking for a place to smoke protected from the late-morning sun. The sun on this spring morning was hot and shade helped. I got that, but every inch of peninsula property was sacred. The sheer number of Charleston tourists demanded respect for property boundaries, or our residents would have no rest from intrusion. I had often heard the frustrations of Charlestonians about the numbers of tourists, but until then, I had not understood.

Our trespasser was an attractive young man in his early thirties. His skin was clean, and he twisted his hair into chin-length dreads not typical of homelessness. His simple shorts, cotton tee, and flip-flops might have meant that he was staying near us; maybe he was a couch surfer crashing with a friend or family member.

The look on his face when we surprised him meant he knew we belonged to the house. The joint in his hands was not too alarming, considering what went on around here regularly. I was long past my inborn, Southern, Bible-belt opinions on smoking a joint. Judgments only waste energy.

I released the need to set this young man straight. If one of my dear neighbor ladies had seen him lounging inside our gate, I dare say they'd have verbally run him off. He must not have been here long.

As quickly as we noticed him, he disappeared down our side street, Carondolet. We were well within our rights to call the authorities, but we opted to let it go.

Greg smiled and said, "I guess I need to get that gate closure welded and installed before too long; I am sure he would not have come into the courtyard if it had been closed."

"Just like the brick they tossed through the window last Christmas. If the courtyard had been secured, it might not have happened." Surprisingly, I was not worked up about the intruder. Except for my initial shock, I was too numb from the inundation of other house issues to get worked up.

I did mention it to my mother later that day.

"Denise, this is not good," she said. "He may be scoping the place out to come back later. What if he jimmies your door looking for things he can pawn? I bet he's done this before and knows your pattern of being away." Mom's voice sounded worried for us.

"Yes, Mom, that could be true because we go to an early church service every Sunday morning."

"Perhaps your routine gave him a sense of security. He could also be coming inside your steps for a smoke break," her voice dripping with sarcasm.

"I know you are afraid for us, but I can't get all worked up about it." I dropped the subject and went outside to pick some fresh lettuce from our garden for lunch.

Early each spring, Greg planted our courtyard garden and filled it with vegetables. We shared the fresh food with everyone on our street. Before we got to landscaping, we liked the idea of a community venture to bring us together. Tomatoes, cucumbers, peppers, and greens were showing off their fruit. During the local Greek Festival, patrons passing our house stopped to examine the garden. I felt proud.

I was giving today's visitor a pass, but I pressured Greg to get our gate post installed, so the gate would click closed. If the gate stayed closed, it would be less inviting for someone to enter. That gate still moved out over the sidewalk and then into our courtyard, depending on how the wind blew, as it did when we purchased the house. Up till that day, the gate had been a lesser priority.

Instead of napping, Greg spent the afternoon working in the back of the house. Finally, he stood next to the central floor joist and called out, "Denise, come back here. It's big news."

"What's going on?" A little concerned, I joined him.

"I am done underneath the house, and our whole floor system is covered with subfloor. No more holes in the floor."

I threw my arms around Greg, and tears dripped off my chin. Two years after our permit was issued, Greg had closed up the entire floor.

We'd had no idea the years of anguish we'd endure to get to this day, some of which would continue. Our Charleston Cottage was becoming our haven, a place we could be proud to share with others. This little piece of history we were learning to treasure was one step closer to completion.

I still get emotional thinking about the day the floors were sealed and the toll of that process on both of us. I had skated into this adventure thinking, *We've remodeled before. We've got this.* In fact, I'd had no idea how low our living conditions would sink—at times, one step above homelessness.

Days later, we cleaned and installed the reclaimed flooring purchased from the 1950s James Island home and placed them throughout the center of the house. As I scraped each piece of flooring, and Greg nailed them in place. Closing the floor and installing the hardwoods and a gate closure formed a ray of hope. We were making progress.

What about You?

- Was Denise's emotional response to the raccoon in the house within healthy limits, or was she being unfair? How would her response toward Greg have affected you? Your spouse? What are some alternatives to how she dealt with the raccoon?

- Has there been a time in your marriage when circumstances affected your relationship?

- Was the house worth their sacrifice? Would your spouse agree? What would you do in their situation?

- Greg and Denise had a role-oriented relationship. What do you think of roles in a marriage? What are your roles?

- What do you think of their interaction after work? Greg said little and went to work to plug holes. Was this OK? Should he have communicated more with Denise?

Chapter 6

It Only Got Worse

*A*FTER GREG CLOSED THE FLOOR system, he turned to the roofline. Our architectural design showed a pitched roof over the current leaking flat roof built in the 1940s. This got tricky because the roof could not be removed and replaced in one day. Greg didn't always explain these particulars to me and perhaps for good reason.

I discovered the truth about the hole in the roof just before bed that night.

Greg stood with his hands at his sides looking up at the sky just inside the back door. Our sons were playing video games after a long day of demolition. It was good of them to help their dad with this large job.

I stepped up behind him with a hug and whispered in his ear, "So, when were you going to tell me we'll have a 10-by-10 hole in our roof overnight?"

"I was kind of hoping you wouldn't notice . . ." He shrugged. "Maybe hoping to ask forgiveness and not permission."

I pulled away. "Seriously? Are we taking assigned watch for the night?"

He turned to face me. "I should have told you but stop with the fear tactics. We will be fine. Promise."

"Look around, Greg! Everyone out there"—I jabbed my finger toward the street—"assumes you have a goldmine of pawnable tools in here. If someone realizes the payoff is worth jumping our back fence, we're in trouble. Home invasion while we sleep in our beds. How in the world are we going to sleep tonight like this? It's crazy!"

"How in the world are *you* going to sleep," he shot back. "*I* plan on sleeping just fine."

"I need to check into a hotel. I am not going to get a wink of sleep."

"Denise, do you trust me? Do you believe I can take care of us?"

"It's not a matter of trust. I'm doubting whether you're being realistic. Bad things can happen with the best plans."

"No one knows the room is open. Our gate is high in the back and there are no two-story windows looking down into our backyard. Let's go outside to the street and look at what they are seeing. Then maybe we can get some sleep."

I quietly opened the front door, not wanting our grown sons to know about our conflict. Greg was right behind me. Walking down the steps to the street, I believed that Greg must be naïve about theft in this city. Just a month earlier, someone had stolen a car on Carondolet. Even our locks deluded us into thinking we were safe. This roof thing was making me crazy.

We stood on the street and looked up. Nothing looked out of place.

"See, I'm right. A flat roof is hard to see, so one would suspect it's open."

Darn. Greg was right, but I didn't want him off the hook that easy. I stayed quiet.

He continued, "Coast Guard helicopters may see our open room, but they'd have to be looking at just the right time."

I looked up and down the street. On Friday nights, there were usually a few folks out celebrating the week's end, laughing and socializing at the other end of the street. But not this week. The area was dark except for a few streetlights and an occasional pedestrian or passing car.

I let out a breath like deflating a balloon. "OK. I guess I can give you that. Please, promise me this'll be done tomorrow. My blood pressure is sky high over this stuff."

"I can get it done with the boys here to help me."

Greg hugged me, and I pressed

CONSTRUCTION BREAK
Seek Wisdom

If we as a couple are on opposite ends of the emotional/logic spectrum, it's easy to see it as a disadvantage, a barrier to connecting. However, if used properly, this can be an advantage. The goal lies somewhere in the middle between logic and emotion because that is where wisdom lies. To insist your spouse move to your side of the spectrum is emotionally unhealthy. One type is not wrong. If you are logical, then you need to have someone help you feel emotions such as loss or anger. If you are emotional, interjecting logic keeps you from over emoting or intense anger.

my head into his shoulder. A moment later, we entered the courtyard, and the gate squeaked.

I murmured, "I used to hate this sound, but on a night like tonight, it's our secret alarm if someone enters the courtyard. I'm actually starting to like it."

We settled into bed, and I finally dozed off around midnight. Suddenly, I came wide awake at 3:00 a.m. The house was dark and quiet. I moved out under the opening in the roof and sat in a cloth sling chair, staring up at the moon. What an unusual experience to sit inside your house and stare directly at the moon. It calmed me. We miss so much, spending our lives under a roof. When my head nodded, I crawled back into bed and slept like a baby.

In the morning, Greg and our boys set the trusses, sheeted the roof by midafternoon, and waterproofed the wood with black tar paper. By evening, the house was once more secure. If only it would stay that way. Every time I thought all the holes were plugged, more showed up.

The weekend after the dramatic roof repair, I woke up with the need to spend an overnight with my mom upstate, about three hours away. I talked to Greg about taking time away. He was planning to demo the bathroom wing, so he was happy to be working solo without my dramatics. Before I reached the interstate, he had a large portion of gypsum pulled from the walls.

Just a few weeks prior to that, Greg had finished our guest bath and extra shower in the laundry room. Days later, the ceiling of the main bath fell in. I shuddered thinking about what might have happened if we had still been using that bathroom. The leaks had rotted the roof and ceiling board, until it finally gave way.

That night after supper with Mom, my phone rang. It was Greg.

I was eager for news. "So, how's it going, dear? Are you finished tearing out?"

"First, have you had a good visit with Mom?"

"Yeah, it's good to be in a complete house for a change. Are you waiting to tell me something?"

"Well, I have a proposition. I need to decide what we are going to do with this side of the house."

"What do you mean 'this side of the house'? What's wrong besides the missing ceiling in the bathroom? And don't forget the creepy feeling you get in there at night."

"Yeah, so you say . . . you and your ghosts. I tore off the sheetrock out there, and the walls are completely rotten from water dripping through the old roof. I don't think I can fix them. I thought I could extend the height of the walls by adding in framing, but it's just too bad."

I couldn't stop my sarcasm. "That adds what, another year?"

"If I am going to do it right, I have to tear off these rooms. I'll tear off this whole side this weekend. I can't build back until I have it off, and I might as well start."

"Do you need me to leave Mom and come home? I can stack debris for you."

"I don't want you to get hurt. Enjoy your mom, and I'll demo the wing. See you Sunday." With that,

Greg hung up and was gone. I envisioned him immediately ripping off sheetrock and knocking down walls. I couldn't imagine him getting all that down by the end of the weekend; it would be daunting to say the least.

I finished the weekend without giving it another thought, though when I pulled onto Congress Street on Sunday night, I couldn't believe my eyes. Rotted wood neatly stacked in a flat pile filled the entire courtyard to eight feet high. Just behind it, Greg was stapling the entire side of the house with blue tarp.

A small group of neighbors stood on the sidewalk across the street, talking in soft tones to each other.

I had no words. I simply went inside to find a broom and dust cloth so I could get the place clean enough to fix us some dinner. We ate and went to bed without much conversation. What was there to say?

Early Monday morning, our fence had a bright orange sticker. A fine! Someone had reported us to the city for the debris.

I read the notice. "Greg, did you know about this Charleston city rule? Can they fine us?"

"I didn't know homeowners need a dumpster on-site. I thought that was only commercial. I guess I was wrong on that count."

Heading inside to grab my keys, I said, "I have time before my first client. Let's run down there."

An hour later, Greg posted the permit, and the dumpster arrived.

That afternoon as I unloaded the luggage that was

still in my car after the weekend, a short, plump lady with a cute face stepped off the porch across from us. Up until then, we had not spoken.

I smiled when I noticed she was headed my way. "Good afternoon. I'm Denise. I'm so glad to meet you."

"I'm Renee, Denise." The lines around her eyes crinkled when she smiled. "I had to come by and tell you, that man of yours tore off the side of your house yesterday. I've never seen anything like it. He stacked each section as it came down. His crowbar and sledgehammer were just a-flying. He's a one-man show, he is. The whole neighborhood sits out on their porches and cannot believe their eyes. And you're usually out here helping him."

"I offered to be here on Saturday, but he wanted to throw the wood and felt I would be a moving target. He said to stay at my mom's. I'd just be in the way."

"He's doin' it his way, and I get that. He's doin' a great job, he is. That house was the worst on this part of the street until you came. I'm surprised it can even be fixed. Every weekend, he keeps pluggin' away, and you got to respect it, you do." She nodded.

"We're sorry it's taking us so long, Miss Renee. Y'all have been more than patient."

"If you do it ya self, then it's done right and as you like it. I get that . . ." Just a tad taller than I, she gazed into my eyes with approval. "You stand by your man, sure do. And I love watching y'all. You take your time. Lord knows, it stood here for years and years in that condition. What's a few years to get it right?"

"That blesses my heart. Thank you for coming over. Miss Renee, if you need us, come by anytime."

As we parted ways, I couldn't help but wonder if she also heard our rather loud discussions.

If only everyone on the street would reach out to us like Miss Renee did. From time to time, others made complaints about the project taking too long and the constant mess, including whoever had turned us in. But then again, I had to admit, three rooms stacked in the courtyard might qualify as too much debris.

That evening, we both carried wood and stacked the dumpster until it was full.

The next day, we had a knock at the door. A tall, young construction worker stood smiling down at me. He was clean cut and obviously not homeless, so I took a chance and opened the door. All I could think was, *Now, what?*

"Can I help you?" I asked, shortness in my tone.

"Hi, I am Daniel. I look for old Charleston wood to do fine furniture and other woodworking projects. Here is my card. Could I rescue some of your wood from the landfill?"

"Wait here just a minute. I'll need to ask my husband."

Gingerly, I latched the door and walked back to find Greg. He was out back assessing his next mode of attack on the project.

I came close to Greg and whispered, hoping the young man couldn't hear our conversation. "Someone wants wood from the dumpster."

"Tell him it's all rather rotten, but he is welcome

to look through it as long as he leaves it stacked neatly and level with the top. Did you get that? I don't want to have to redo the dumpster, and the requirements say nothing can be sticking out the top. They will charge us more."

Daniel stood expectantly waiting for the verdict as I slowly cracked open the door.

"My husband is fine with you sorting through it, but you have to leave it organized and below the top of the dumpster."

Daniel didn't hesitate. "Oh, sure thing. Thanks for letting me go through it."

In less than an hour, the woodworker removed a large pickup load from our stack. I was thrilled to have additional space for more debris.

Greg spent several weekends cleaning up the soil and figuring out the new foundation. In the end, this decision to demolish the wing added forty-two square feet to the bedrooms, and we ended up with a brand-new addition.

A few weeks later, I felt out of sorts and lounged on the sofa in my comfy pants with my laptop, thinking about a cup of tea. I was in a mood that day, a mood I didn't quite understand. Maybe it was my client load, maybe the house . . . who knew? I was just not myself.

Greg came in from his job. "That work function is tonight, Denise," he said.

I groaned. "Why do I need to go? They won't miss me this one time."

"It's better when you are with me," Greg said,

pulling out his trump card. "I need you at these things, Denise."

"All right. All right. I'll go, but it's not like I am dying to parade about and schmooze all night. Promise me we'll stay for only an hour and then we'll head over to our supper club. Usually, I enjoy dressing up and a night out, but tonight I am at a low. Mingling with this Charleston business crowd means being on top of my game, making meaningful conversation."

"Maybe this will do you some good and put you in a better mood." Greg was encouraging, and I knew he wanted me by his side at social functions.

I quickly changed into a dinner dress and freshened up in front of the mirror. Crow's feet and dark circles around my eyes reminded me I was not sleeping well. After some makeup to cover the truth, I grabbed my handbag, telling myself, *You can do this.*

Greg put his arm around my waist and drew me to him. As I hugged him, I focused on the current state of affairs—the unfinished flooring, lack of window trim, tools piled on an industrial shelf along the wall. Were these the cause of my off mood?

He released his grip. "I know this is not how you want to spend your evening. Thanks for doing this for me."

I kissed him and put my head on his shoulder. Socialization was not his thing, and I helped ease his pain a bit.

"I am not sure what it is with me right now. I'm working on trying to come out of my funk. Maybe it's about the mess here. It's affecting me more than I'd care to admit."

We set the security alarm and made our way over to the event. On the drive over, Greg agreed that we would spend the obligatory hour mingling with his colleagues and then head to a monthly supper club I coordinated each month. I planned to hold Greg to this deal. He'd rather be with our friends too. Greg was quiet, and I decided to let silence fill the drive. I was not in the mood for a deep discussion.

Stepping into Greg's world of the architectural and commercial building community of Charleston was usually a good time. It was a change of pace because I worked as a solo practitioner with revolving clients. Due to my legal constraints of confidentiality, Greg wasn't privy to my work. Our professional lives couldn't have been more separate. Yet I believed we had never been more together than we were right then.

This house with holes had wiped away our game faces and exposed us for who we were. At the same time, it had brought forth strength we had not experienced in almost three decades of marriage and was forcing us to rely on each other.

We arrived at the venue and registered at the entrance. I pasted my right shoulder with a printed name tag.

The venue was part of the Mt. Pleasant Memorial Waterfront Park overlooking the Cooper River. The lights on the water sparkled. We chatted with those we knew, circulating around to catch our acquaintances scattered throughout the room. I made a concerted effort to contribute to the evening and stay by Greg's side.

After a decade in Charleston, I was familiar with a majority of those present in the room. After a while, my six-inch heels were getting the best of me, and I decided to retreat to a nearby porch rocker. I looked at my phone, happy to see that it was only fifteen minutes before we could leave.

As I sat, barefooted, in the chair, I saw a slender, dark-haired beauty enter the room. I didn't recognize her but thought little of it until she scanned the crowd and headed directly to Greg. She was dressed in a form-fitting black suit that showed her figure, and she carried herself with confidence that exuded a sexy energy.

Greg's face lit up when she reached him. I could tell immediately they were well acquainted.

Many people stood between me

CONSTRUCTION BREAK
Protect the Relationship

Marriage does not ward off strong physical and emotional attraction for other members of the opposite sex. After all, we are human. Marriage is a vow to forsake all others. By stepping out, we may have the delusion that things will be better with someone else, but we will assume new shortcomings and take ours with us. If we indulge in the temptation, it may be our own insecurities leading us there; the enemy knows our weaknesses. The best deterrent to an affair is a conscious effort to keep out of compromising situations.

Respect each other; take care of your own inner life. Give your partner the benefit of the doubt, knowing that truth will prevail and any breach will come to light. Be compassionate by putting yourself in your partner's shoes and do not let anger fueled by fear wear away the intimacy of the relationship.

and their conversation, so she and Greg didn't notice my attention. As they talked, I noted their heartfelt laughter and the ease between them. She leaned her head toward him as if to emotionally rest on him for stability. This was more intimate than I had ever seen Greg with a colleague.

I couldn't hear their banter, but when she laughed and reached out to him, I imagined her saying something like, "Stop, Greg, stop. I cannot take anymore."

My hackles rose.

They both looked down and then back at each other.

Suddenly, Greg caught himself and glanced around. He stuffed his hands into his pockets. She reached out to touch his arm and pulled him back into their conversation.

I sat in the chair, dumbstruck by what I was witnessing. My mind ran circles around the possibilities. My thoughts were raging. *What the heck is going on? Why don't I know who this person is? How long has he known her? I have to get ahold of myself! After all, this is Greg my loyal, most trusted husband. How long has she been his "friend"?* All these and more swirled around in my head.

I tried to decide what to do next. *Should I go up and break into their conversation?* I already felt off balance, so this was the last thing I needed. In an attempt to calm myself down, I paced my breathing. Breathing helped. Isn't that what I told my clients?

As I observed the cues between them, my mind shot off fireworks. I imagined myself kicking her butt. But we weren't in a bar. This room was filled with the source of Greg's livelihood. His reputation was at stake. Besides, any type of confrontation would have been senseless without the facts, not to mention embarrassing.

I wrangled my thoughts into a more logical tone. I knew my deep love for Greg did not mean becoming overly possessive, but jealousy was coloring my judgment. I was not on my A-game that night.

As my pulse slowed, I acknowledged that, at the very least, Greg was validated by their relationship and, like me, he was allowed to have friends. I reasoned that she must be a colleague without enough importance for him to mention her to me. Yet my own insecurities, the endless stories I heard about infidelity from my clients, and my vivid imagination created a perfect internal storm.

Greg was generally a closed book to others and rarely showed his feelings, even to me. And now he was laughing and connecting with a hot woman in a tight dress.

I was jealous. Their connection scared me. After all, I was the one he should share his soul with, not her.

Surely, Greg was guarding himself so he would not be drawn into an emotional attachment. I knew in my heart this was true, but my logical mind was taking a holiday.

Suddenly, a karma-induced message swelled inside me. *You deserve this. You are guilty of the very same thing.* And I remembered . . .

What about You?

- Could Denise control her initial reaction to seeing Greg's interchange with a coworker? If not, what was her best recourse?

- Was Greg wrong in any part he played in the interchange with his coworker? How could he have made this easier for Denise? Should he have had to?

- Is one of you more jealous than the other? Is insecurity an issue with that person?

- Have you ever been attracted to a member of the opposite sex after your vows? (This does not need to be verbally shared.) Is attraction within our control? Are there coping skills to handle unexpected connection?

Chapter 7

WHERE THERE'S SMOKE, THERE'S USUALLY FIRE

TWO DECADES EARLIER, AT A similar business event, I had walked into a company Christmas party in a borrowed cocktail dress. Greg had been with that firm only a year, and I was nervous. I was afraid I'd say the wrong thing or look ridiculous. The venue in historic downtown Greenville, South Carolina, was a restored Victorian house with an expansive entry lavished with Christmas greenery and lights.

Couples gathered in small clusters throughout the room, all dressed in glittering Christmas finery. I immediately picked up on the aroma of prime rib. One young attendant walked throughout the room with a tray of oysters on the half shell; another had a tray of bacon-wrapped asparagus.

I helped myself to one of the oysters then paused in front of the bar, choosing something sparkling and spiked to settle my nerves. Turning back to the room with my drink, I saw a tall, handsome man in an equally handsome navy-blue suit with a brilliant white shirt.

On his arm was his lovely wife, blond and almost his equal in height. Together they circulated through the room with the charisma of a political candidate.

They were strangers to me, so when I returned to Greg, I leaned in and whispered, "Who are they, Greg?" with a slight movement of my head in their direction.

"Micah is one of our project managers in the Hendersonville division. That must be his wife, Sylvie. He's a former professional football player."

Sipping my drink, I followed his progress. He was one of the most handsome men I'd ever seen. And more importantly, his confident swagger showed he knew it. As out of place as I was in this setting, Micah was in his element. He was the total package.

They made their way around the room before reaching us. Minutes after meeting them, I learned they had two daughters about the age of our sons and their third child was on the way, though in her cocktail dress, Sylvie looked anything but pregnant.

CONSTRUCTION BREAK
Attraction is Uncontrollable

Attraction is the primal part of us that is unexplainably drawn to another person like the atoms of our cells are drawn to one another. We can see ourselves touching that person intimately. We might look at them and imagine it—hands caressing, lips devouring—you get the idea. We need to have some measure of attraction to make the relationship viable. It can grow overtime, and it can be damaged due to outside influences, but attraction is paramount to having our sexual needs fulfilled. As we age, we see the person who was and the body and soul we connect with, but attraction is built in those early days.

As the dinner bell rang, Micah stepped to the chair next to mine. I focused on the china and wrinkled my brow. *Really? What is he doing?* My plan was to fade into the background and say little, but it didn't take me long to find that Micah was on a mission. With one question after another, he monopolized my evening.

"What exactly do you do, Denise?" he asked.

"I gave up my job with Fluor Daniel three years ago to stay home with our three children until our youngest, Megan, goes to school. How long have you been with Waterman?"

"Just two years. Last year, our founder moved me nearer to the mountains to be the project manager over the large homes we are building outside Brevard."

"That's why I've never met you in the office when I've stopped in. I thought I knew everyone; it's a small company."

"Are you from South Carolina, Denise?"

"Yes, but only since the age of twelve. When my mother married a southerner, he brought us to South Carolina. It was a hard adjustment in middle school, but I love it now."

Micah's intensity was unnerving since his wife flanked his other side. I kept hoping he would concentrate a little more to his right. As the night moved on, he continued to zero in on me.

On our ride home, Greg brought up the couple.

"Micah is a sharp guy, don't you think? So handsome and smooth. I saw you two talking over dinner, Denise. If I was a jealous person, I might be a little mad."

"No way. He's smooth and good looking, but I'm not sure that is such a good thing. There is something about him that doesn't sit right with me. I am upset you didn't at least try to rescue me."

"He's all right, Denise, really. It's not like you'll see him outside of the occasional Christmas party or other work gathering. You haven't seen him up to this point all year."

I put it out of my mind. Greg was right. When would I ever have to deal with Micah? The company party was done for the year. Thank God.

The next morning just after 8:00 a.m., the phone rang. Greg had left for work, and I was busy in the kitchen getting breakfast for my brood.

"Hey, Denise, it's Micah Barrett. Has Greg gone already?"

My heart moved to my throat. *All year he hasn't rung our phone, and now he's calling the house.*

"Good morning, Micah. Sorry, you just missed him; he's on his way to the office."

"I was telling Sylvie last night we would love for you to come over for dinner. We could have drinks around the fire pit and get to know each other better. Of course, Greg's included in this." I heard him lightly chuckle.

"I'll mention it to him." *Greg can come too? Nice.* "Try Greg at the office. I'm sure he will arrive anytime now. Bye now." I hung up the phone. Was it my imagination, or was this a bit too coincidental? I loved Greg, and we got along as well as a young married couple could with the stress of three children under three. What if Micah caught me at a point of weakness?

When Greg got home that evening, it all spilled out. "He is nice enough, Greg, but I'd rather not hang out and get to know him." I didn't want Greg to know I didn't trust myself to linger a little too long in conversations with that handsome man. The best thing to do was to avoid him altogether.

"Fair enough. I'll just make excuses and never bring it up when I see him."

Months passed. Micah called the house rather randomly, making up reasons why he needed to talk to Greg. One afternoon, I went into the Waterman building to drop off something for Greg. Micah was in Greg's office sitting across the desk from him. He was tan and lean in his business polo, looking picture perfect. I was so shocked to see him, my voice cracked when I tried to say hello.

I handed Greg the envelope he was waiting for.

"Hey, girl, it's been a while," Micah said. "How ya doing?" He looked squarely at me. His thick Tennessee accent was charming.

"I am good, thanks." Speaking as dryly as I could and still be polite, I looked away as soon as I acknowledged him.

"I was just asking Greg how a frog like him got a beauty like you, Denise."

I sensed the pink rising in my cheeks. I wanted to run out of the room, but I was too stubborn to give him that satisfaction. Who did he think he was, sweet-talking me right in front of Greg?

"I guess I got lucky." Greg smiled and chimed in, seeing I was in trouble. I gave him a look of thanks and headed out the door.

As a young woman, my own mother had been drawn into an affair with someone at work. It cost our family so much that the very memory of her consequences kept me on the straight and narrow where Micah Barrett was concerned. Micah started showing up at our house from time to time, but as quickly as he arrived, I sent him packing. After months of providing unwelcomed attention, Micah eventually left me alone. Greg never admitted the seriousness of the situation, and I still carried the feeling that he could have done more to protect me.

～

From my chair at the Charleston Christmas party, I watched as Greg finally moved away from his animated conversation and looked through the crowd for me. Perhaps it was my turn to rescue him. I decided to approach the two of them with the intent of debunking this jealous spirit inside of me. That was my full intent as I headed toward them.

Greg reached for me as I drew near to the lovely woman he'd been engaged with the last few minutes. "Brittany, this is my wife, Denise. Denise, Brittany Barber."

"Denise, so nice to meet you. You know your husband is sensational . . . right?"

I grinned at her and looked at him with no response. Instantly, Greg knew he was in deep trouble with me. At the same time, I recognized that she was doing this of her own accord. He could not control what she was saying. I knew this from my own past experience. It'd been a few years since I'd felt jealousy, but old habits die hard. I noticed Greg was reading all of this on my face.

She said, "I have worked with Greg over the last year on a project for the hospital system. We're still a few months out from completing it." They continued talking, and I was lost in my thoughts.

Affairs of all varieties were my business in the counseling office. A man in a bit of midlife crisis begins to work around a woman ten years his junior. They have much in common professionally and share a deep, mutual respect for each other. Maybe both are at a lull in their relationships and, in a moment of weakness, a line is crossed. A few, like Greg, believe an affair could never happen to them. Those are the ones who fall hardest.

I offered Greg an exit strategy. "We have a dinner engagement across town in just a few minutes. Greg, it's about time. Nice meeting you, Brittany."

Without waiting, I walked out ahead of Greg. In the parking lot, I turned to him and, in a heated voice, began. "So, you have a *friend* you know quite well. I couldn't believe what I was seeing between the two of you from across the room. I'd call that flirting if I didn't know you better."

"She's an owner representative, Denise. That is all you saw."

"You've been to lunch together? Multiple times?"

"No, I promise. It's a professional relationship, and she's married. I am *not* doing anything!"

The conversation halted. In that moment, I knew Greg was telling me the truth, but I couldn't help but sink into a bit of depression. Was he tired of me? Why wouldn't he be? I was exhausted with the weight of the renovation, the constant mess, and most of all, myself.

At the supper club, Greg mingled with the men and I with the women. Our drive home was quiet.

After we were inside our Charleston Cottage, he said to me, "Denise, you know you are my girl, right?"

My heart melted when he reached for me. He pushed me against the unfinished wall and kissed me like I had not been kissed in quite some time. He spent the rest of our evening letting me know that no one was coming between us.

Nothing else mattered.

～

By the end of the third year, we were both experiencing burnout where the house was concerned. Our daughter got engaged and her wedding date was just six months later. Life was moving on with or without our house complete.

We wanted Megan to have the wedding she'd dreamed of, meaning much of our renovation funds went toward wedding expenses—the

CONSTRUCTION BREAK
Physical Affection

Sex starts in the morning. Our physical connection throughout the day ignites a passionate desire for each other. There is no formula, but touching and valuing each other are central to physically connecting. If you are not naturally affectionate, meeting your partner's need for reasonable touch is part of reaching across the aisle and loving well.

dress, the wedding coordinator, the party rental, the photographer—and a thousand other details.

We rented a large home on Lake Hartwell to house extended family from out of town, dusted off our boat from storage, and played most of that weekend, water skiing and tubing like old times. All and all, it was a welcomed retreat for Greg and me, a reminder of what life was like before Congress Street.

After the wedding, a heaviness descended on both of us when we stepped back into the house. Greg had the bedroom and bath wing closed in and ready for tile and flooring. He had spent the weeks prior to the wedding finishing the outside of the new addition with siding, paint, and trim, so our homeowner's insurance would approve our coverage for the year. If the outside was finished, they didn't care about the inside.

Greg tried to stay a few steps ahead of both Charleston city inspectors and our homeowner's insurance. The building permit would soon expire, so we researched how to comply with their stringent requirements. Charleston was the magnificent city it was because of their attention to detail. Their historic preservation required intentionality with ordinances and codes to keep it that way. The city of Charleston allowed us to keep our permit active. I sensed they were glad we were saving a piece of history because there were many Charleston Cottages on the list for condemning.

One night not long after the wedding weekend,

I arrived home and smelled smoke throughout the house, but I dismissed it as one of our neighbors grilling steaks outside. I began to think about what we would have for dinner and decided to start the charcoal grill myself.

I never got that far because as I moved through the kitchen, I noticed smoke forming inside the center of the house. I frantically ran throughout the house, opening the doors to the laundry room, the bedroom wing, and even the attic. Nothing.

Something was terribly wrong. I pressed Greg's number at the top of my favorites list.

"Greg, smoke is building at the center of the house. I can't see where it is coming from. I have been over the house again and again. I've been in the courtyard and backyard. Nothing."

"I am turning on Rutledge now," he said. "I've got less than a minute." I imagined him pushing on the gas pedal in a rush to get to me.

I hung up and waited on the steps.

I heard Greg's pickup accelerate, saw him slide into a street parking space, and jump out of his truck, barely shutting his door. He looked both ways and crossed the street, yelling to me to turn on the hose bib and pull the hose to him. He ducked his head under the porch.

"Hurry, Denise! I saw flames running on the ground right here under the porch as I drove up."

As I ran, I yelled back, "It's one of the only places I think I didn't look." I dragged the hose down the side-walk to the courtyard, praying we were not too late.

"Do I need to call the fire department?" I asked as I handed him the sprayer.

"Give me a few minutes." Greg leaned under the piazza and sprayed. Smoke billowed. In less than five minutes, Greg dropped the hose.

It's out." Greg leaned back on his heels, weak with relief.

"So, no fire department? What if it is in the walls?"

"Let me check more thoroughly. Unless it's absolutely necessary, I don't want to stir up drama on the street and have the fire department punching more holes in everything."

Greg crawled under the porch and investigated where the flames were centralized.

He emerged and pounded dirt off the knees of his khakis.

"It's out! If it had been seconds later, the fire might have gotten into the foundation. We could have lost the house—a total loss with dry balloon framing. God protected us tonight." He pulled me into a quick hug. "Give me a few minutes to poke around to see what caused this, and I'll be in shortly. Sit down and breathe, Denise; you look white."

"I cannot believe how close

CONSTRUCTION BREAK

Outside Forces

Outside forces pull on the marriage unit: in-laws, money, children, friendships, work, and loss. Keep them at bay by limiting their influence on you as a couple. Develop a feeling of walking together, hand in hand, tackling each life stressor together as a team. Standing united is important to keeping a balanced relationship, each of you having the same amount of power and voice.

this was."

I paced inside the house while Greg tried to determine the cause. Sitting after such an adrenaline rush wasn't an option right then."

Greg opened up the wall of the small kitchen pantry where our chest freezer was plugged in, then crawled under the house. He worked on the fuse panel on the porch and came back in with his observations.

"The original knob-and-tube wiring ignited at the freezer plug. I think over time it overheated. It means a long night for me. I'm going to disable all the knob-and-tube left in the house tonight. We have a new service for the addition and back half of the house, but I haven't had time to switch the front of the house over to the new service."

His shoulders sagged. "It could have cost us the house. I shudder to think of it. Just because the wiring worked for ninety years doesn't mean it can handle our modern appliances. I have to know we're safe before sleeping in here one more night." He was near tears. "I hate to think what might have happened."

My voice was calm. "God spared the house. The timing couldn't have been more perfect. I'm sorry you have to work the rest of the night to get it switched. What can I do to help?"

Rarely had I seen Greg shaken, and tonight he was trembling. It was my turn to be strong for him.

What about You?

- Can you relate to how Denise's past behaviors colored her judgment at the business event? Was Greg's female colleague demonstrating signs of "Danger up ahead," or was Denise overreacting?

- Was she right to trust Greg, or did he need to prove himself further?

- Affairs in the workplace are prevalent. How do we protect our marriages in those settings?

- When Micah was pursuing Denise, did Greg stand up for her in a way that validated his love? Was it right for Denise to ask Greg to stand up for her?

- Have you had a similar experience? Does it remain a sore spot or is it resolved?

Chapter 8

WEEDING THE COURTYARD

*B*LACK METAL SPIRES POINTED HEAVENWARD to enclose gardens and homes in this holy city were a tribute to Philip Simmons, one of the artisan blacksmiths who left his mark across Charleston for more than fifty years. When we came upon our 1929 Charleston Cottage, that wrought iron was the first thing we saw.

Our squeaky gate defined the corner of Congress and Carondolet Streets. The classic lines of those spires spoke of Charleston artistry and helped me look past the sagging and worn structure. We could only hope our gate and spires had been molded by Simmons or one of his talented apprentices. Our iron was a smaller, more humble version of gated court-yards east of the Crosstown.

Inside our beloved boundary stood what, at first glance, appeared to be a tree. Jeffery, one of the locals, shared that in his fifty years living in this neighbor-hood, this tree had stood as part of the landscape. Looking closely, we saw that it was nothing more than an overgrown bush with multiple stems mistaken for branches. Over time, the branches had intertwined with parts of the wrought iron and offered shade for the western side of our house. Rusty nails protruded from the bush's trunk. Blight covered the leaves. A rope—most likely a former clothesline—had grown through the bark.

After reaching out to a Charleston tree specialist about what to do, we were encouraged to remove the bush and replace it with a small tree known to grow well in our hot climate.

One Sunday afternoon, our son Ethan came for a visit. He saw Greg digging around the stump in hopes of clearing it from our courtyard. However, that bush was not leaving without a fight. Ethan found a shovel to help his dad work. For over two hours, they worked to expose more and more of the gnarly roots, hoping to break the bush free from the soil.

Sweat dropped from their faces until, finally, Greg inserted a crowbar to lift the root ball. After much heaving, Greg piled the tangled web on the sidewalk to be hauled away. The dirt left behind was dark and sandy, perfect for gardening.

We then had a blank canvas.

The next day, I was back in the courtyard, weeding away, preparing to plant for spring. I stood and leaned to stretch my knees from squatting. I was thinning the heirloom canna lily bulbs beginning to emerge. In a moment, I sank back down and then continued until noon. My garden hat now shaded my face but gave little protection from the sun blazing down my neck and back.

Finally, I stood and stretched, wiping my brow on my sleeve. Pulling off my gloves, I laid them on the piazza floor. A brisk walk would do me good. The wrought iron squeaked, and I moved to the street.

Gerry, our neighbor at the end of Carondolet, called out to me. "How are you doing this morning, Miss Denise?"

"Working hard on the front. I can't wait to plant some stuff."

Gerry was one of my closer friends on the street. She and her mother Shirley had lived in city housing at the end of Carondolet for more than two decades—longer than most other residents in the area.

I waved and turned from Race Street onto Rutledge, walking at a quick pace. At the intersection of Rutledge Avenue and Calhoun, a small tan pickup truck passed me, slowing to stop for the red light.

My heart rate picked up.

I know the man in that truck.

More than ten years had passed since I'd seen him, but that man and that truck were branded in my memory. I knew him . . . and his dark secrets.

Standing at the crosswalk, I stared at the stoplight with the truck in my peripheral vision. More than anything, I wanted to hide, but the landscape was bare. Not a single tree or post stood nearby. It was OK. I didn't think he'd noticed me.

I was amazed at my degree of hypervigilance, like a part of my brain had suddenly opened up a file that had been neatly stored in its recesses. The sight of him retrieved it in milliseconds. The lady waiting next to me had no idea the mental gymnastics playing inside my head or my difficulty in getting my emotions under control.

Seeing him so unexpectedly, so suddenly, also helped me realize how much healing had happened since we'd last met. I would not allow him to trigger a relapse to debilitating anxiety. Not that day, no way!

I focused on steady breathing. That dang light was taking forever.

~

Ten years before, I had been thrilled to be the newest faculty member at McGregor Elementary School. With my three children in that school, our schedules harmonized perfectly. Moving to Charleston was our latest adventure. I was ready for the change, though I missed my mom and sisters who were more than three hours away.

My interview with Dr. Sands, the administrator, went smoothly. My graduate degree from his own alma mater, my past experience in second grade, and my references were a perfect match for McGregor. I was hired.

The first month of school was a steep learning curve for me. My supervising teacher was a micromanager, and I kept longer hours than in my past years of teaching. One particular afternoon, I remained in my classroom well after school let out. Since the school was open because the Boy's Club met in the same facility,

I used the time between 4:00 p.m. and 6:00 p.m. on Wednesdays to catch up on planning and grading papers. Greg and the kids went out for pizza to give me this time.

Working at my desk, I was startled to see Dr. Sands leaning against my door jam. I wondered how long he had been standing there. Smiling, he stood erect. "Denise, are things going well? Are you settling into a routine?"

"Yes, thank you. I think I am getting the hang of it. I wish my early routines were a bit more structured, but I'll know better next year."

"Good to hear it. Just hang in there. It does get easier." He raised his elbow in a nervous gesture. "By the way"—he grinned and looked into my eyes—"you sure clean up nice."

Uncomfortable, I stood and pulled my canvas tote bag to my desk. "I have to meet up with Greg. Thanks for coming by to check on me."

Over time, Dr. Sands's compliments became commonplace. They seemed harmless enough. After all, the man was old enough to be my father. He was happily married to a very attractive woman who worked in the front office. I told myself he was only being friendly, nothing more.

In my mid-thirties, my appearance was rather plain: no makeup, little jewelry, and simple clothing. Attracting the attention of any man other than my husband was the furthest thing from my mind.

I loved the school. They pushed for academic excellence, yet they extended freedom to their teachers to be creative in the classroom. Their stellar reputation in the community drew many local residents and stationed military families to place their sons and daughters at McGregor.

However, the administration placed high expectations on the staff. Along with the academic strain, they examined our tests regularly. Our professionalism was continually under scrutiny.

At the end of the first year, Dr. Sands called me into his office for a closed-door meeting. The week before, one of our church friends approached Greg about working as a subcontractor. That news had reached Dr. Sands, and he called me in to say, "Going into business can be hard on your marriage. It creates a lot of pressure, and the marriage takes the hit."

My face grew warm. "Thank you for your concern. We will consider that."

I left his office indignant and upset. I felt invaded, and he was creeping me out. However, I kept my opinion about Sands to myself. I was afraid of retaliation. I buried my doubts deep, making sure nothing slipped out in my conversations, even to Greg.

By April of my second year at McGregor, I was experiencing stress-related health issues. I simply could not fulfill all the demands of my classroom, deal with strained interactions with Dr. Sands, and also care for my family. Always an overachiever, however, I was determined to dig in and make it work.

Each school day, my free period was the same hour. I would leave my classroom to enjoy the peace and quiet of the teacher's resource room. I worked on classroom prep, but mostly it was a place to clear my head.

One afternoon as I sat at the table grading papers, Dr. Sands opened the door and stepped inside. Immediately I felt nervous tension. Something was weird with him.

He grinned his usual grin and moved closer and closer to me at the table. "Hey, Denise. I see you are getting a few minutes to yourself."

Tension oozed from him. I kept on writing.

School rules advised us to never be alone with members of the opposite sex. Here Dr. Sands was intentionally violating his own rule. Soon behind me, he suddenly rubbed his hand up and down my back. Up and down, moving on my back with more intense contact.

I stared at the page in front of me, hoping he would leave.

His cheek almost touched mine as he bent over me. I could feel his breath in my ear when he whispered, "Denise, I've been very concerned about you. I can tell you are under a great deal of stress. You've missed several days this quarter. You look tired, and you've lost some weight. We do care about you and want to be there for you, but you have to let us know what we can do."

A shiver of revulsion sent a spasm up my spine where he touched me.

Eeeww!

His face was so close to mine, I dared not turn and look at him. Within seconds, I closed my notebook, gathered my papers, and pushed my chair back. I had to get away from him.

"I am fine, really. Just fine!" My voice cracked. *What did he want from me?*

Heart pounding, I dashed out of the room, trapped in a horrified replay of his breath in my ear. It felt surreal.

Somehow, I pushed back the turmoil inside me and finished my school day. Looking back, I have no idea how I got through it. My kids didn't notice my dripping tears on our way home that afternoon. By the time Greg got home from work, I mustered enough willpower to bury it deep in my soul. I kept it from Greg.

But at night trying to sleep, my thoughts raced. *Had I led him on? Was this somehow my fault? Should I tell Greg?*

If Greg went ballistic, I'd lose my job. Our kids would have to leave school. Dr. Sands was secretary of our state school association. He could blackball me so I'd never teach in this state again.

I felt such shame that I decided against telling anyone. *Pretend it's not there. Pretend it didn't happen.*

A few weeks passed. One afternoon, my mom was on the phone, and I spit out words in a jumble like a wooden tower of blocks tumbling to the table and cascading over the floor. I told her everything.

Mom was irate. "That back rub was very sexual. You have to report this."

"I don't want to tell anyone. It happened a few weeks ago, and I have told no one, not even Greg."

"He should have *never* under any circumstances put his hands on you, Denise. He's your boss, and you're twenty years younger. That makes his actions even worse. Rubbing your back and whispering in your ear? Think about it."

"Maybe I blew this up in my mind, and he wasn't really making a pass at me." I started to cry. "I try to be discreet. I don't wear revealing clothing. Could I have led him on?"

Three hours away in Spartanburg, Mom's voice sounded very close. "Denise, this is not your fault! You could wear a gunnysack and still be attractive."

I pulled a tissue from my box. "Elliott came back to me in that moment, Mom. I felt that same creepy, sexual feeling from when I was seven." Elliott, my stepfather, had been inappropriate with me once when Mom was away. That dirty, worthless feeling had come rushing back.

Mom said, "You need to tell Greg. He'll be there for you. I know it's embarrassing, and you are afraid of

CONSTRUCTION BREAK
Feeling Duped, Look Deeper

A foundation of mutual respect for the other person should carry us through after the disappointments of the relationship come to light. Dating life, if honest and long enough, should expose some of these problems. Perhaps your respect has been damaged because you feel lied to by your spouse. You think, *I would have never married them if I'd known.*

In the normal, stressful day-in and day-out, we are laid open, and shame and guilt can emerge. But there is a growing hope of being seen in our inmost being and feeling accepted and even validated in that place. We look for a way to reduce the conflict between us, but all we can control is our own attitudes and responses. By choosing to understand each other, we can reduce the immediate frustration and open ourselves up to connection. By considering the other person's deeper need, we extend grace and earn the right to speak the truth of our own needs.

how he'll take it, but Greg loves and trusts you."

Tears streamed down my face. "I'll look for a good time to tell him. Thank goodness summer is just a few weeks away."

Summer arrived as a welcome escape from the problems at McGregor. I filled the weeks with activity and, most of all, enjoying my children. As the new school year approached, all that I buried from the year before grew like a pit in my stomach.

A week prior to the first day at McGregor, the teachers in-service training with Dr. Sands began. A few days into the training, I was in my seat when my body began to feel clammy, my head dizzy. My pulse raced, and I couldn't catch my breath. No matter what I did, I couldn't get the episode under control. A fellow teacher drove me to the emergency room.

The doctor came into the room and shook my hand. "Mrs. Broadwater, what you experienced is a panic attack. I suggest you see your family doctor." He handed me an envelope with a few pills inside. "Take one of these if you have another episode."

I stared at the doctor in disbelief. "Panic attack? Now, they will say I am nuts?" That feeling started out my third year, and I continued to fight panic a few times per week.

I made an appointment with my family doctor.

After conducting tests for my heart and blood-work, Dr. Baughman believed I was dealing with trauma. He gave me a more specific medication to manage my anxiety and urged me to consider what unleashed such a reaction.

The next day, after the kids were in bed, Greg and I were in the family room alone. I moved over to sit close to him, "Greg, I have been having panic attacks because of something I should have told you about months ago."

"What is it? What happened?" He was immediately on high alert.

I filled him in on that day in the teacher's lounge.

Greg's face turned red. "I want to go down there right now and deck him! In today's world with all the protocol we have to avoid even the hint of sexual harassment; this is a deliberate act."

We talked about options, about the kids' schooling, and what we should do. Finally, I said, "I'm going to see Dr. Baughman tomorrow. Let's see what he says."

That night, I slept easier for the first time in months.

The next morning, I entered Dr. Baughman's office, afraid to hear the test results. Was it my heart? Would I need to go to the hospital?

When Dr. Baughman entered the room, emotion washed over me. Sobbing, I told him the whole story.

He slowly replied, "That was straight-out disrespect for you as a woman. There is no justification for it. It triggered your past trauma." He handed me two fresh tissues. "Your heart is fine."

I managed to say, "What can I do? I need to finish my contract." *Please give me something that will stop the turmoil in my head!*

"Continue the medication, and let's get you into counseling. You might be able to finish the year.

However, if your panic attacks continue, I'll write a letter to relieve you of your obligation to the school. Does that sound like a plan? See me in a month, so I can check on you."

I walked out of his office and marveled that I could be so out of control of my own body. Up until that point, I had been hoping sheer willpower could solve this.

I continued teaching and started weekly sessions with a therapist. Over the next seven months, I realized my days at McGregor were over. More than that, if this story got out, I'd probably never teach again—at least not in this state.

I planned to leave at the end of the school year without giving a reason. I feared the backlash from my coworkers and the humiliation for my family. I doubted whether confronting him was worth it, and I preferred to slip away quietly.

The school year was nearly done and so were my therapy sessions. From the first session, I knew counseling was the right course of action for me. Over those months, my counselor and I cleaned out many areas of my life, like pulling weeds and thinning the undergrowth. I ended my sessions with a fresh perspective.

In early May, new contracts came out, and word soon spread that I was not returning. Soon afterward, a fellow teacher stepped into my classroom and blurted out, "You're leaving because of Carl Sands aren't you?"

I held my breath for a moment, then tried to play it cool. "Sarah, why would you say that? I just can't keep up this pace anymore."

She moved closer to me. Her blond hair gleamed under the lights. "Come on, Denise, I know something has gone on with you. It's obvious to anyone paying attention. Have you considered you're not the only one he's done something to?"

"What? He has had issues with other teachers? Here?"

"It's been a while, but I believe he was charged with rubbing a teacher's back and messing with her bra."

Tears welled up, but I pushed them back. I'd been through seven months in a therapist's office, and I knew this was my personal secret. It wasn't the right time to spill it here.

"I cannot discuss this right now. I just can't."

Sarah gave up her quest and left my room.

The moment she'd gone, I closed the door.

I laid my head down, and I cried. I cried for that awful day in the teacher's lounge. I cried for my kids who would have to leave their friends. I cried for the little girl inside me who, long before, had needed to scream, *"It's not OK!"*

I went home feeling spent, wondering how I was going to continue my teaching responsibilities.

The next day, Sarah was at my door the minute the children were dismissed. I was not happy to see her.

She was excited and talked fast. "I spoke to my tenth grade son last night. He told me Dr. Sands comes into the halls at the high school and ogles the girls in between classes. It is so obvious; the kids call him a perv behind his back."

"Are you serious?" For the first time, anger replaced

my pain and fear. I thought of parents entrusting their children to this "safe" school and having that trust violated. Everyone knew of his habit of meeting with high schoolers behind closed doors.

I drew in a shaky breath. "Sarah, this is incredible."

"Well, he's got an issue. The last teacher was blamed for misinterpreting his affection . . . whatever that means."

Enough. I told her of the back-rubbing incident.

Sarah's mouth formed an *O*. "That's almost identical to what the other teacher said."

I said, "I cannot slink out of this school if children are potentially involved. I have to tell someone who can do something about it."

"Meet with Jim Cosak, the associate superintendent," she suggested. "Jim is a reasonable, caring man. Dr. Sands and Don Hickman, the superintendent, are as close as family, so Don probably wouldn't be as approachable. Maybe Jim would mediate the meeting."

That evening, Greg agreed we should set up a meeting with the associate superintendent and ask him to speak with Don and Dr. Sands.

The next day, Greg and I met with Jim and learned he, too, was leaving our county board. He was sympathetic and thanked me for working through my contract under these circumstances. He organized a meeting that included six school board members—all men.

When Greg and I entered the room, they were all seated around a conference table. They placed us at the end along with Don who conducted the interview. Dr. Sands sat across from us with the others flanking him.

Don asked me to tell my story, and I gave them the details.

When I finished, Don said, "Denise, don't you think Dr. Sands was simply concerned about you? You had been sick, and he was trying to convey that he cares about you as part of our school team? We looked at your interview and know you had a difficult childhood; maybe you misinterpreted his affection."

I shook my head. "Isn't there a rule in your employee code against men being in a room alone with women, much less physical contact between the sexes?" I glanced at Greg, who had a grim set to his jaw.

Going on, I said, "For months I tried to convince myself Dr. Sands's behavior meant nothing. Any trauma I went through as a child does not affect what he did. You all have a responsibility to see that the teachers and students here are respected and not violated."

More rebuttal came from the group. Finally, Greg stood up and pointed his finger in Dr. Sands's face. With much resolve and a bit of anger, he said, "You put your hands on my wife. There is nothing more to say about it!"

Dr. Sands's face turned white.

We both got up and left the office without another word. When we pulled out of the school driveway, we knew our life would never be the same.

At the first stop sign, I leaned over and hugged Greg. He was my protector. I understood that in a new way that day. We were soon celebrating our tenth anniversary, and his strength that day in the office bound us in a way nothing had up to that point. After all my work for healing over the past seven months, those few minutes set me on the path to spiritual rest.

In the end, it was the word of Dr. Sands against mine, so the issue never went further. I filed reports in the appropriate places should my case help someone else, and that was all I could do.

After leaving McGregor, I enrolled in a graduate program to get my second master's degree, this time in clinical counseling. I then became a licensed counselor with my own practice in Charleston. Thousands of men and women have passed through my office with similar stories of grief and trauma. God helps me find light for them when the path is dark, to find their voice and cry out, *"It's not OK!"*

As I stood watching the tan pickup truck pass under the green light, I felt a rush of energy. I knew who the man in that truck was. But, more importantly, I knew who I was.

What about You?

- Denise came from a difficult past, and she was compromised at work. Early in their marriage, she wasn't open with Greg immediately. Would you have been offended if your spouse told someone other than you about something this serious? Do you offer and accept unconditional love? Do you believe in it?

- Might Greg have felt tricked if Denise hadn't been open about her past? Can we ever fully know someone?

- Does this piece of information about Denise explain more of her makeup, her insecurity, and jealousy tendencies? Do you ever consider your spouse's story in how they relate to you?

Chapter 9

COINCIDENCE OR
DIVINE PROVIDENCE?

ONE AFTERNOON WHILE DOING ERRANDS on Johns Island, on a whim I stopped at Habitat for Humanity's ReStore. This particular store received construction donations from Kiawah and Seabrook Island. Why not check it out? Maybe they would have something we could repurpose for our project.

In the back area, I came upon a set of maple cabinets piled together in a room. I browsed lightly and wondered if I should bother with it. Greg was adamant that he had no intention of reconfiguring cabinets. As I examined the pieces, a volunteer taped up a picture of the original kitchen. Their professional team had deconstructed this set, meaning that these cabinets were undamaged, and all the parts were nicely packaged.

The doors were a simple shaker style, an exact match to what we were pricing at the custom kitchen store. The clean lines were modern and simple. The only drawback was that our plan called for white cabinets. These were bird's-eye maple, a caramel-colored hardwood.

I texted Greg: "ReStore on Johns Island has cabinets that appear to fit our plan down to the turntables in the two corners. I'll have to stand down a little old lady walking around me trying to check them out. If you hurry, I might avoid a purse over the head for standing in her way."

He immediately texted back: "I can come now."

As I waited for him, the white-haired lady saw my determined expression and moved to another area of the store. When other patrons appeared interested, I ran interference. I was not about to lose this opportunity.

Greg arrived minutes later, tape measure in hand. He inventoried the cabinets one by one and found that the pictured kitchen was complete except for one drawer. We asked, and a volunteer found the drawer in the back room.

Still holding his tape measure, Greg scratched his head with the side of his hand. "What a great find. It will fit the space almost exactly to our plan."

I went into action. "Let me ask the price." I hurried to find someone in charge. I saw a bearded man wearing a reflective vest headed our way.

He said, "Four hundred fifty dollars, and the sale is final."

I texted Greg and craned my head to see his response from across the building. He gave a thumbs up.

I opened my purse. "Where do I pay?"

"At the counter there." He pointed then headed

off. "While you take care of that, we can start loading them into your truck."

Receipt in hand, I walked back to Greg. We shared a knowing smile. As if God had placed this perfectly matched set of maple cabinets in ReStore on the rarest of mornings when I was passing through Johns Island.

I followed Greg home, then returned with him to pick up the second load. Feeling astonished and a bit overwhelmed, we sat quietly on the drive home.

Greg broke the silence. "There are a few extra cabinets. I'll cut one down for the guest bathroom as additional storage and convert the desk to a rolling island."

Greg stacked the cabinets into our tiny living space. He removed our temporary setup and spent the next weekend installing the maple cabinets. As they went in, I watched the kitchen materialize, nothing wasted or redone. He used the double-oven box as panels under the bar. By the time the last piece was installed, only six inches had been added to the center of the kitchen.

The following week, Greg researched the process for making concrete countertops. He ordered a bullnose form to use for the edge and gathered the materials. He had extensive experience finishing concrete but forming floors and foundations were very different from crafting a countertop.

After nine bags of cement and an intense day of mixing several wheelbarrow loads, our concrete countertop was finished. Greg spent the week sealing and polishing the surface. The gray stone was cool and smooth. If I hadn't seen him pour it with my own eyes, I'd swear it had come from the earth.

After four years, our kitchen was workable and nearly complete.

～

Shortly after her wedding, our daughter, Megan, had accepted a position in Portland. She came to spend a weekend with us before the big move, and I wanted our time together to be memorable. We'd shopped King Street all afternoon and stopped for tea and pastry at St. Albans, a retro French-style café where Congress met King Street.

Megan took a sip and peered at me over her porcelain cup. "Mom, I don't know how you've managed. I mean, open floors and that gross bathroom ..." She picked at her scone. "I'm worried Dad is working too hard. He's basically built a new house in an old shell." Her twentysomething face crinkled with concern. "You aren't so young anymore, you know."

I held back a laugh. "Dad and I are healthy and strong. Hard work keeps us going." I grew serious. "What worries me is you, going all the way across the country. No more weekend visits."

"It's not like it's forever, Mom."

I didn't reply, but I knew how life could take hold and not let go. Portland might be like that for Megan.

She went on. "Dad said you had an incident on the street last week."

"We were getting dressed for bed around 10:00

p.m. when a big boom sounded outside. Dad pushed me to the floor and yelled for me to lie still. He said it was a large caliber handgun, very close.

"I got my cell and called 911. Apparently, several of our neighbors were on the phone with them at the same time. We didn't know if another shot was coming our way, so we stayed down until sirens told us the police had arrived. The whole thing was over in ten minutes."

"That's just crazy!"

I chuckled. "Dad says bulletproof sheetrock might be the board of choice for the walls facing Congress." I touched her hand. "As the street has new families come in, this will get better. It's already a lot better than when we first arrived."

"Did they find who did it?"

"A .45 caliber gun casing was on the street, and they believe the shooter was in the driveway of the vacant house not but ten feet from our corner." I sighed. "A Kiawah architect just closed on that house. They'll begin renovation sometime this year."

Megan whispered, "What would we do without you and Dad?" Panic hovered beneath the surface.

"Honey, it's going to be fine. This is exactly where we are supposed to be. God's with us, and we are safe."

We left our dishes on the tray table and headed down the sidewalk. Megan slipped her arm through mine, something she hadn't done in a while. She was leaving, and she was a worrier.

We passed a young family pushing a baby stroller. A couple on bikes headed toward the Battery. A college-aged long-boarder slid past us. All of these spoke of positive change to me.

One Saturday morning, Greg lay in bed watching *This Old House* on PBS. It was almost 9:00, and I wondered if he was planning to make the weekend count. Each weekend we failed to work was another week added to the finish line.

"What are the plans today?" I asked.

"I don't know. I think I'll sleep today. Can't I get a break?" He rolled over and groaned.

I headed to the kitchen to start a pancake breakfast. That would surely draw him out. Pans clattered and doors thumped, maybe a tiny bit too loudly.

Greg got out of bed and came up behind me. In my ear, he said, "It makes me feel so bad when I cannot give you the things you need, Denise. You get that, right?"

I curved my mouth in a sad face and nodded. I turned to hug him for a long moment.

He was burned out with the reno, but aside from the extra work with building projects, I still needed to clean the kitchen, go to the laundromat, and scrub the bathroom. Who wasn't doing those things on a Saturday morning after the pancakes had been eaten?

An hour later, we headed outside to finish a french drain, so we could start on our back steps. We hardly got started when the rumble of a thunderstorm and a spray of drops sent us rushing for the house. We barely made it under the awning before the sky fell. The roof roared with the downpour. This type of interruption tended to put us both in a bad mood.

Since we had plans to attend a friend's art drop-in later that day, we made our way there earlier than expected. The artist was displaying handblown and painted jewelry in a shop on Church Street near the famous Charleston market.

I was amazed at the quality of the workmanship in each of the displays and found several one-of-a-kind pieces to keep and share. As an added bonus, we walked around the historic house and admired the design and workmanship. In years past, this building had been a general store. Now, it was the perfect studio for the owners to do their art and architectural drawings.

After we enjoyed friendly introductions and completed our purchases, the sun came out. Greg wanted to get back to his project, so we moseyed home.

While he measured twice and cut once, I grabbed a broom to sweep our sidewalk facing Congress Street. I was pulling together the dirt and leaves from the city's crepe myrtle tree at the front of our house when a young man ambled around the corner from Senate Street.

When I saw that he was approaching me, I held my breath. *Now what?* Drama was the last thing on my wish list for this day.

His face showed immense relief when he saw me. "Are you Mr. Greg's wife?" he asked. He stepped into my personal space and reached out his hand in an imploring gesture.

I looked for a way out but found none. His unwashed aroma hit me.

"How can I help you?" I held my broom between him and me.

"Ma'am, I'm homeless and in such a bad way this morning." He placed his hands on his hips and breathed a deep sigh.

My walls began to come down. I could see he was hurting. "Are you hungry? Can I get you something to eat? Some water?" He wasn't as dirty as some of the homeless people I see.

"I am that, ma'am, and that'd help me. But I could really use a bar of soap and a facecloth to wash up, and I need to wash my clothes."

"Let me see what I can get together for you. Wait here." I smiled to reassure him that I would help. I relaxed my broom weapon and started for the gate.

"While you look, let me help you finish sweeping." He extended his hand.

Hoping I could trust him, I handed him the broom and slipped inside the creaky gate. "You don't have to sweep," I called to him. "I'll be back in a minute."

The gentleman insisted and began sweeping where I had left off.

I hurried inside and scrambled around for a few items from my pantry: protein bars, tuna pouches, beef jerky, and a bag of cheese crackers to help with some carbs. I grabbed a bar of soap, a washcloth and hand towel, an old pair of Greg's socks, and one of his T-shirts. I found a few dollar bills and coins in the change jar I kept for the laundromat. I put the money in a sandwich baggie and the rest in a plastic grocery bag.

I rushed back to him and, seconds later, I saw the gratitude on his face, the lightness of his step as he strode down the street.

What touched me most was the look on his face when he first came around the corner of Senate Street. He knew if Greg were out working, he would have compassion on him.

That morning's storm had upset our plans, so I was out front sweeping the sidewalk at just that moment. This meeting was no coincidence.

I stepped inside to place my broom in the utility room and dropped into my chair. Suddenly, I was sobbing so hard I could barely catch my breath.

Greg came in for a drink of water and saw me falling apart. He knelt down next to me, and my story poured out. My heart said, *Stop complaining. I have a clean bed, healthy food, and a warm shower. And more than that, my family and friends love me enough to take me in if I need help. Sure, the house doesn't have all the amenities. Sure, living this way gets tiresome at times. But what does that really matter? I am rich in what matters most.*

After my meltdown, Greg stacked his tools in the makeshift closet and took me out to finish the day with drinks at Tavern and Table and a few minutes outside enjoying the waterfront of Shem Creek.

I relaxed, enjoying the atmosphere.

While we were sitting close and cozy, I brought up something that had been on my mind. "Greg, would you consider having a mason repoint our fireplace? It's a big job. A mason would have it done in a couple of weeks."

His voice sounded testy, though not as strained as usual when I brought up the topic of subcontractors. "I hate to pay someone and end up disappointed." Greg looked intent, wondering where I was going with this.

I went on: *This Old House* used the American College of Building Arts on their Charleston project for both their wrought iron and brickwork. They have a website. I'll reach out and see if they'd come out to see the fireplace and the wrought iron." I was asking and not pressing too hard. The reno was our project but ultimately his call.

"I'd be OK with that."

"Really? OK, I am shocked, but thank you for giving this a try. We can at least speak to them."

I knew the concession Greg was making by releasing our fireplace to a brick mason. Refurbishing the fireplace himself would mean another eight weekends of grinding the mortar and repointing the joints.

"Do you want dessert before we leave?" he asked.

"No, let's get home. I have to write that email to the college before you change your mind."

Greg chuckled. "Yeah, that's probably about right." He rested his hand on my leg and leaned in for a little public display of affection.

Construction Break
Finding Our Balance

Marriage does not merge us into one being; rather we are two trees planted side by side in a wood. The two form their own family and continue to grow as two separate trees whose branches and roots intertwine as time goes by. They grow toward the sun (God) in spiritual growth; they preserve water and share minerals; they withstand the raging storms that encircle them. Each tree brings balance to the other.

1. Too much overlap = stunted growth.

2. Too little overlap = disconnection and greater vulnerability to outside forces.

3. Between the two trees, seedlings grow. The seedlings are nourished and protected until uprooted to another wood.

What about You?

• Is one of you more empathetic toward the other? How do you define empathy?

• Denise continues to press Greg for added help with the house. Greg didn't like to ask for help for various reasons. Is there a time to speak up and challenge your spouse's issues? Why or why not?

• Could you use a goal to work on together?

Chapter 10

MURDER BEFORE BREAKFAST

*T*HE COFFEEPOT MADE A SPUTTERING noise. I picked up my travel mug and stared at the dripping pot. I had a 9:00 a.m. client and was scrabbling to leave. Every morning had the same scrambling, but I didn't understand where the time went.

As the final drops of black gold fell, the screen door squeaked, and then I heard *rat-a-tap, rat-a-tap.* Someone very determined knocked on our door.

My heart jumped a beat. No one ever stopped by this early. "Greg, someone is at the door!"

He called from the shower, "See who it is before you open it. Yell through the door if they look suspicious."

I opened the blinds on the door's window and peered through the dirty, wavy glass. I liked a clean window, but this section of porch was original, and it stayed covered in street dirt, the dark sand constantly blowing through Charleston's streets. It stuck to every house, every car, and every pedestrian. I had first felt street dirt on my face on a New York City sidewalk, but until I moved to the upper West Side of Charleston, I didn't realize most cities have the same sooty dust. Similar to their fight on crime, the city of Charleston had put some effort into cleaning up the streets. It helped only a little.

A somber man in a blue uniform stared back at me through the glass.

I turned to shout toward Greg, "It's a policeman!"

I figured he was about as safe as they come, so I opened the door and spoke to him through the rusty screen. "Good morning, officer." My voice sounded weak. "What can we do for you this morning?" I could tell by his grim expression that something bad had happened.

Behind him, a crowd of first responders gathered across the street, surrounding Dawson's house two doors down. Dawson worked at the Medical University of South Carolina, known locally as MUSC. He had been one of the first neighbors to welcome us after we moved here.

"Oh, my," I gasped. "Is everything all right?"

"I can't go into details, ma'am, but I need to know if you or anyone else in your house heard anything at all this morning. Any commotion or unusual noise on the street?

"I didn't hear anything. Let me ask my husband, and I'll get right back to you."

I hurried to Greg who had just come out of the shower and filled him in on the situation. "The policeman wants to know if we heard anything unusual this morning."

"I didn't hear anything," he said. "Did you?"

"Me neither."

The officer turned and left the piazza, moving up the street. I couldn't imagine what must have happened and put it out of my mind. I had seven counseling clients on the schedule for the day. For my clients' sakes, I had to focus. With a quick prayer for Dawson's family, I drove away from the flurry of activity.

In my rearview mirror, I saw two officers stretch yellow tape across the street, cordoning off my home and several others. Whatever had happened, it was serious, and it was right outside my door.

The TV reporter said an assailant had come through the teen's bedroom window with the intent of taking him out. It appeared premeditated, which in some awful way gave me a bit of comfort that this wasn't a crime spree in which we could be next. The reporter went on to say the young man had been a model student at a local college with his whole life ahead of him.

For a brief moment, they flashed the teen's picture on the screen. I froze. This young man rode his skateboard on our streets, laughing and hanging out with other teenagers. He often waved and said hi when we passed each other.

Surely it couldn't be him who had died. But they kept saying the attack was earlier that morning in our neighborhood. He had been stabbed in his bed and bled to death on the way to one of our local hospitals.

While we were choosing our clothes for the day

and making coffee, a young life had drained away. I felt sick.

In tears, I called Greg. "I am pretty sure Dawson's son was killed this morning, Greg." My voice broke, and I couldn't go on. I pulled a tissue from the box on my desk.

"Oh, man. I hate that for him." Greg then fell silent.

Finally, I gasped, "How should we handle this? Should we go over there? We only met Dawson once, but . . ." I choked up, thinking what if our own sons, Ben or Ethan, were taken from us in such a violent fashion.

"We can decide when I get home. Try not to get too upset, Denise. God will give us the words and show us what to do." Like me, Greg wasn't prepared to deal with all this emotion while at work.

Late that afternoon, I reached home and had to park a block away. Friends and relatives gathered on Dawson's front lawn. His house was a bit larger than ours, and the yard had room for grass. I recognized a few faces. Most of all, I felt a wave of abject grief rising from them as they hugged each other and wept.

Dawson was a friendly man who knew everyone. With a stream of porch sitters who waved and spoke to us from his yard on a daily basis, he shared the purest form of culture in the neighborhood.

Fitting the key into my front door, I knew Greg would want to go over there. He always took the high road. It might not be comfortable because of our newness to this neighborhood, but it was the right thing to do. My own Amish heritage said I should carry them a meal, but we were still lacking so much in getting one prepared. Instead, we put some bills into a card, a symbolic gesture that seemed so small compared to this tragedy.

When Greg got home, we walked across the street. I had a knot in my stomach, fighting to keep my composure. Listening to hard things was part of my work as a counselor. I have listened to grieving parents more times than I can count, but I still felt the pain of loss every time. Beyond a therapist, I'm a wife, a mother, a daughter, and a sister. That day, I was a mother with two boys who were just a little older than Dawson's son.

As we walked, Greg, my rock, tried to help me hold it together. "Dawson is our neighbor. We need to reach out and tell him that we care and are praying for his family. At the very least, we need to acknowledge his loss."

"I feel like we're intruding," I said. "Everyone there is either family or longtime friends. They've loved this young man since he was born."

Sympathy card in hand, we reached the crowd, and they made a path for us. When we reached Dawson's gate, a short man with a mellow voice said, "Hi, I am Curtis, Dawson's brother."

Greg spoke up, "We have a card for Dawson, Curtis, to let him know that we are thinking of him, and we want to be a help in any way we can. We know this is a hard day, and we are glad for someone to give it to him if he's not able to come out."

Curtis reached out and took my whole arm in his. "They would have us be against each other, black against white, but Martin Luther King said we all bleed red, miss."

Tears came down my cheeks. "We realize that we moved into your neighborhood, but we have felt nothing but kindness. It has meant so much to us. We cannot begin to imagine what you are all experiencing with the loss of this young man."

The front door opened, and Dawson walked out. His eyes were bloodshot, and his face puffy from crying all day.

He walked straight to Greg and embraced him. Everyone fell silent. Weeping, Greg said, "We're so sorry. We are praying for you. If you need anything, please don't hesitate to knock on our door."

When Dawson took the card from Greg, he tilted his head back, searching for words. Finally, he said, "Mr. Greg, ain't nobody in this neighborhood going to mess with you, sir. We see what you carry on your back into that house." Suddenly, Dawson laughed out loud. Greg laughed, and then the crowd laughed, breaking the tension.

Dawson said, "You a one-man show. Yes sirree, a one-man show. I have done construction all my life. You are a trip to watch."

Wiping his eyes, Greg smiled and said, "I do what has to be done. If you need anything in these coming weeks, we are just across the street. We aren't just saying it, we mean it."

Dawson embraced us both and watched as we

made our way through the yard filled with men and women of all ages. We shook hands with several as we left through his gate.

I was so glad Greg encouraged me to step out of my comfort zone and make a small gesture. My heart swelled. This was no longer "the neighborhood." Now, it was home.

Within a month, Dawson packed up and moved. He never stayed in the house overnight again after his son was taken. The intensity of the trauma and the senseless loss of his son made staying impossible. The cottage lay dormant for almost a year.

After the funeral, friends held vigils and Mayor Joe Riley visited. Dawson constantly faced the memories. I understood his need to leave the area. I could not imagine the loss of a child who had barely started to live.

After Dawson's house was sold, it underwent a full remodel. The vigils ended. The news reported only an occasional update on catching the murderer. The case fell silent.

When we worked on the weekends, people passing by often stopped to chat. Miss Renee made a point to wave and speak whenever we were outside.

Later, she admitted she had been watching us for several months but was too shy to say hi. She reminded me of my own mother—also named Renee—a single woman with several children and grandchildren, living out her retirement years alone. Her knees were bad, and she got lonely for her children who lived in other states. Miss Renee had a sweet smile, but don't try to take advantage of her. She'd lived the school of hard knocks.

"Miss Denise, you need to speak up if they are putting debris on your corner," she told me one day. "Don't let them do that, now. You don't rent here; you are a homeowner!"

I smiled. Her feisty ways and generous spirit warmed my heart.

"The neighborhood is changing with each passing day," she went on, looking down the street at several construction dumpsters—evidence of more remodels then in progress.

"Yes, it is, Miss Renee. When we get a bit more done, I want you to see the house."

She grinned and showed the wide gaps in her teeth. "There will be time for that. It's good for Greg to take his time. He does all his own stuff, and it looks beautiful. Just the way he likes it." She turned toward the street, saying as she went, "Yes sirree, Congress is coming up!" She moved back to her piazza and sat in her chair. I returned inside to help clean the jobsite for Greg.

Yes sirree. Congress was coming up. We felt privileged to be a part of this new, blended community.

What about You?

• Greg and Denise encountered a tragedy on the street and felt the need to reach out to their neighbor. Greg gave Denise the strength to overcome her insecurity and make the connection. Do you help your spouse in an area where they are less than confident? Do they let you?

• Losses can pile up in a relationship. What are some of the losses Greg and Denise have experienced in this story? What losses are you carrying? Have you laid them to rest or are they still a weight on you?

Chapter 11

OUR END WAS EXPOSED

WHEN GREG TORE OFF THE end of the house, displaying our beloved front room to outside scrutiny, I wasn't prepared for the fascination shown by our neighbors. Some on bikes, others walking hand in hand, slowed down to steal glances into the house's interior. A few stopped to stare. Everyone wanted a peek at what was inside like a big reveal on *Fixer Upper* and *Flip or Flop*. At times I wondered if we are living less flip and more flop.

The front of the Charleston Cottage was different from the rest of it. At some point in its history, someone had smeared a thick coating of stucco over the original siding from the top of the gable down to the sidewalk. We wouldn't know what hid behind that section until Greg pulled it free.

Greg opened the ceiling, and a squirrel's nest came tumbling down on top of us. Early in the project, Greg had tacked up metal screens when we heard scurrying above. For months, we listened to them insistently chewing, hoping to get back in. Very soon now, their entry would be covered with cement siding. Good luck to the squirrels who dared sink their teeth into that.

By ten in the morning, Greg was high on a ladder, and the living room had a gaping hole at street level. Nellie was an elderly woman who lived a few doors down. She stopped her car in the middle of the street and rolled down the passenger window for a chat.

"Sir, I want to congratulate you on coming so close to finishing this project." She leaned forward so we could see her face through the open window. "What are your plans for this end of the house?"

Greg leaned to peer around the twisted limb of the crepe myrtle tree. "This side will match the addition on Carondolet: cement traditional siding on the main section and cement shaker shingles on the gable."

She beamed. "It is going to make this entire corner look new. This house was an eyesore in the community. You benefit everyone who lives here by your work."

As she idled, traffic backed up behind her.

Greg called down, "We appreciate you taking the time to stop and speak to us. We'll have an open house when we're finished. We'd love for you to walk through."

"I'll look for the invite." Saying her good-byes, she left before the cars behind her started beeping.

Minutes later, a pickup stopped. The driver yelled at Greg, "You're doing an amazing job, young man!"

Greg waved but didn't answer. If he stopped to talk to everyone, he'd never finish before dark.

I replied to the driver, "I can tell you he'd rather be

fishing on a Saturday—something he rarely gets to do these days."

"I know that's right. Well, it is shaping up, and I promise you it will be worth the sacrifice. Have a nice day." His taillights disappeared down the street.

The sun was already bearing down like a weight on my back. Did the guy in the truck have any clue what this house had cost us? Did I? The final reckoning was still ahead.

"Weekends off, that's a novel thought," I remarked.

Greg said, "No one wants free Saturdays more than I, but we need to get these big projects done. Wishing doesn't make it happen."

He inserted his crowbar under wood and dried stucco. A gray shower of dirt and debris fell to the sidewalk. Working in rhythm with Greg, I loaded our truck, fitting in each piece like a puzzle. Greg had trained me to maximize the space, and that day we had more than a full load.

Stucco fell in large chunks, so I pulled out our orange cones and placed them on the sidewalk to keep pedestrians safe. These stucco sections were much too heavy for me to remove, so I stood back and watched Greg work, feeling helpless when I wanted to make the job easier for him.

I got antsy standing there. "If we don't get this debris to the landfill before it closes at 3:00, we'll have to leave it on the truck until Monday."

Greg wiped his forehead and stopped to breathe. He checked his watch. "It's 11:00. I have to get all the sheeting hung to close up the opening before we can leave. That's got to be done. I'm not sure we'll make it, but I'm going to try."

James, a man in his early sixties, rode by on his bike and stopped near an orange cone. He had lived in our house as a child. A handful of times, he had knocked on our door for something to eat to stabilize his blood sugar. Greg had a soft spot for James. So did I.

He had a towel on his shoulder. He wiped the sweat from his brow as he balanced his bike with one foot on the ground. James was an alcoholic, and he had already partaken this earlier in the day.

He stared at Greg then peered into the open end of the house. I slipped inside to get all three of us some cool water. Before James went on disability, he had painted many of the houses in the downtown area. He was a wealth of information and loved chatting about the local goings on.

With Greg still high on the ladder, I returned with water and a few peaches on a tray. The two of us ate while we waited for Greg to come down. A group of young ladies came out of the triplex on the corner of Senate and Congress,

CONSTRUCTION BREAK

A United Front

In marriage, pulling together as a team increases the confidence, trust, and respect at the foundation of the relationship. In this case, Denise worked with Greg, not assuming it was his job to do the front of the house. To the outside world, they were united. Consider your outside world. In-laws, social circle, work, and friends—are they free to divide and conquer in your relationship? Do you present a united front? Consider making these adjustments to shore up the marriage foundation. Loyalties, even within families, should adjust to include a marriage relationship.

and we watched them strolling toward King Street. Although Senate Street had a reputation for being dangerous, its newly renovated spaces were filled with vacationers who walked to King Street for dinner, to the market for shopping, or to spend a lazy afternoon at the beach.

James and I exchanged knowing glances as the young women teased each other and laughed.

I said, "The neighborhood is changing, huh James?"

"You got that right, Miss Denise. Just a few years ago, I couldn't ride my bike down Senate. The men on those porches would beat me up and take my bike."

"Seriously?"

"Yes, ma'am. I saw it done to other guys I know, so I knew better than to try it. You were asking for trouble if you went through there." He bit into his peach, tilting his head back to catch the juice.

"It was still bad after we moved in," I told him. "We didn't drive down that way. Most of the gunshots and police issues came from Senate. Now look. Renters headed out for lattes, families with small children; they're a common sight."

"It is hard to believe unless you see it with your own eyes." He looked up at Greg. "Sir, you plan on getting this closed up by dark?" he asked with a twinkle of laughter behind his eyes.

Greg called back, "Can I hire you to stand guard if I don't make it?" He chuckled.

James retorted, "You don't get this closed up tight by nightfall, you better get yous a shotgun and sit in this room facing the street. Because they's coming for yer tools; you know that." James laid his peach pit on my tray and shook his head with laughter.

"I know that's right," Greg said.

James was a neighborhood newscaster. Once, we mentioned to him that we had some mail for the Smith family, the renters living there when we purchased the house. A few hours later, the son of the family arrived on our step to pick up the mail. Word got around. Quick.

"My security system monitors these rooms," Greg told him as a way of letting the neighborhood know. "But never you mind, I'll get this closed up this afternoon."

Soon James waved and was gone.

Around noon, I took a quick break to eat some lunch.

I could eat while Greg worked, so I used the break to sweep nails and other debris from the sidewalk. The sun passed over the roof, so this area was finally in shade.

Greg stuffed in his last bite of sandwich and waved me to stop cleaning and to sit down with him. I found a spot on the steps.

He said, "Denise, I have to get this end sheeted now. That means I will be holding the sheets and asking you to shoot the nail gun to anchor them. Once you shoot a few nails, I can let go and finish nailing. Do you think you can handle that?"

Rather reluctantly, I said, "I can try." I hated to work the framing nail gun. It was heavy.

The moment we held the first sheet in place, a

downpour as cold as a mountain stream soaked us both. I hated to get my hair wet because it would instantly frizz, but we had no choice but to keep going. Whining about the rain wasn't going to make the job any easier.

The sky dumped buckets while the two of us worked in tandem to hang 4-by-8 sheets of plywood until the entire end was covered. We didn't take a break until the last nail went in at 2:20 p.m. The landfill closed at 3:00 p.m., and they might not let us in after 2:50 p.m.

We dashed inside to towel off, grab dry clothes, and rush to the pickup. Then we headed out. Our 1997 truck looked tired, but it was willing and able.

We could not go fast, so we chose the quickest route. Praying for light traffic, we breathed a sigh of relief when we pulled onto the landfill scale at 2:45 p.m. Greg was flushed and clammy, drained to the point he could hardly move. We exhaled and relaxed. We'd made it.

Greg patted my hand. "Can you give them our license?"

I jumped out of the truck to get the permit. They knew us by now, and the process went quickly. In two minutes, we moved slowly up the hill toward the dumping zone.

The difference between new construction and renovation is the burden of tearing out the old before rebuilding. When we pulled onto the return scales, the landfill manager told us we dumped sixteen hundred pounds. The more we released from the old, the lighter our burden became.

When we began, we had considered ourselves veterans of remodeling, but this Charleston Cottage took us to places we never dreamed of. It pushed us to the end of our energy, to the furthest reaches of our relationship, and to the brink of giving up. When we returned home from the landfill that day, we had our first glimpse of the treasure rising from the rubble.

This journey had been the ultimate trust game, and we were determined to win.

～

I opened my computer on a Monday morning and discovered an email response from the American College of Building Arts. As one who tended to expect bad news, I opened it nervously.

Their masonry professor would like to come out with an apprentice to examine our fireplace. They were looking for historic projects, and they had extensive experience with Charleston's turn-of-the-century masonry. The professor himself would be overseeing the project and allowing his students to work alongside him. I called Greg with the news, hoping he had not changed his mind.

"Greg, ACBA is willing to do a field trip to see our fireplace. This is amazing that they will even consider repointing it."

He said, "You think it's been dusty up till now, just wait. This is a whole new level of dust." I imagined the quirk on Greg's mouth.

I paced the kitchen, my habit while on the phone. "Please, Greg, do this for us, for me!"

"I am going to remind you this was your idea. Looks like we are discussing mortar joint styles tonight." I heard him clicking his pen back and forth, so he was considering it.

"I like it when you talk dirty. See you tonight." I smiled and laid down the phone.

A few days later, I heard a knock at the door. A broad-shouldered man, ten years our senior and dressed in work clothes, stood outside the piazza door. We were expecting him, and Greg had spent at least two nights preparing the fireplace for his inspection.

We were nervous and expectant as we opened the door.

"Hello, sir, we are Greg and Denise Broadwater. Welcome to our home."

"Andy Solomon here. You contacted our school a few weeks back?"

"Yes, we did." I invited him to step inside the kitchen.

We gave him the grand tour and told him stories of our projects. He was one of the few people who fully grasped what we had been through, so we enjoyed talking with him. The cottage's original siding was

CONSTRUCTION BREAK

Let the List Go

We continually grieve our list of hurts. In arguments, these lists can arise over and over again. They influence the assumptions we put on our spouses. Let your story of hurts go and agree to not rehash it with each other. Write a present story and be patient with each other regarding offenses. We all have differing abilities to release. Over time, we learn our spouse's sore spots. Flexibility in areas that can accommodate is a way to ease the rub.

now shiplap on accent walls in three rooms. The old porch boards were a breakfast bar, and the 1929 beadboard ceiling in the kitchen was fully restored.

Andy said, "This renovation is impressive—old school like my daddy and my granddaddy taught me. I have been working bricks since I was knee high, if you know what I mean. If you entrust me with this beauty," he patted the fireplace, "I'll make it the showpiece of the house." As we talked, Andy pulled some of the mortar loose, examining the situation.

Greg found his photos of some joint styles and pointed to one. "We talked about the weathered mortar joint. It'll show the detail of the brick and give dimension."

Andy nodded. "Good call. I can start next week. Does that work for y'all?"

Greg and I looked at each other. I was buzzing with excitement.

"Sure," Greg said. "I'll hang a plastic curtain surround to keep the dust from spreading. Let me know what else I can do." Greg reached out to shake hands, and we had a deal. I could hardly sleep that night.

After the masonry crew's first day, we came home from work to find dust coating our kitchen lights, counters, and floors. The vacuum for the grinder didn't pick up much dust. Fortunately, the bedroom doors were shut during the day, but some dust had still seeped under the doors.

Hands on hips, I looked at the mess. I had a full caseload that day, and I needed to recharge. "I am so tired."

Greg called to me from the laundry room. "No bellyaching, Denise. I told you what would happen." He came out with an armload of cotton towels.

"How will we get this cleaned up enough to sleep tonight? I'm going to have to change the sheets and wash the comforter."

He dropped the towels into the kitchen sink and turned on the faucet. "I'll start wiping down from the top. When you are done in there, come out and help me finish. The floor might have to be mopped twice." He squeezed out the first towel and pulled the ladder to the edge of the kitchen cabinets.

"When we're done here, I'll tape the edges of the curtain down to contain more of it." He carefully wiped mortar dust from our beautiful bird's-eye maple kitchen cabinets.

As I tore off the sheets, water ran from my eyes, and I'm not sure if it was dust or exhaustion. Hours later, we showered and dropped into bed.

Andy arrived in the morning and apologized for the dust. His air purifier had broken down, but he brought a new one. He said, "This should solve the dust problem—at least most of it."

Thankfully, he was right. Between taping the plastic draping and his new air purifier, the dust was more manageable over the remaining twelve days of the project. Nothing got all of it, but we could manage.

The final day on the project, Andy pressure-washed the brick. That removed years of dirt and cleared away any errant specks of fresh mortar. The original color returned, and it was gorgeous.

Andy looked over his handiwork and grinned. Just as the fireplace had been the center of the home for cooking and heating in years gone by, now it was the central sculpture of our Charleston Cottage. He rubbed the side of the fireplace as though giving it a final goodbye. "Greg, plan to seal the brick to keep it clean. It'll take another ninety years to get that bad again, so this should do it in our lifetime."

Greg nodded. "We love the weathered style joints. It looks like I imagined it did in the 1920s or maybe even better."

The men shook hands. As Andy exited the door, he leaned back in to say, "You start laying your patio, give me a call. We would love to have that project as well."

The moment Andy left our piazza, motivation lit a fire in both of us. It felt like a breath of fresh air. This was the lift we'd needed to keep on working. Greg removed the plastic curtains, and we spent the evening giving the entire place a good cleaning.

The following weekend, he tore down the partition between the two rooms, and light poured throughout the house. At odd times, I found myself standing like a statue in the kitchen, staring into the living room. The house grew by a third that day.

Finally, Greg got started on the last room—the living room. He opened the floor and used two railroad jacks to lift the house off its foundation. The city's crepe myrtle tree had sent a giant root through the foundation, leaving bricks on the ground.

Digging down below the root, he cut it back until it was under the sidewalk. While Greg sawed off the root, I went to the guest room to call his father. Greg's father was elderly, but once a builder always a builder. He checked in on our progress every few weeks.

When he picked up, I started in: "Dad, Greg is cutting back a crepe myrtle root and repairing the foundation brick on the Congress side," I told him, my anxiety coming through. "Will that tree root grow back to lift up the foundation again?"

Greg's father chuckled. "Maybe in another eighty years, but not in your lifetime, Denise."

"Oh, right. I guess I look for things to worry about." I returned to the doorway where Greg was working and told him what I'd done. Greg had to stop sawing to have a good laugh.

I grinned. Yep. My worry often outweighed my logic.

While I visited my mother the next weekend, Greg finished the floor system, insulated it, and put down the first layer of flooring. He was exhausted, but he didn't stop. He wanted to surprise me, so he spent extra hours spreading our living room rug over the unfinished plywood and setting up our comfortable chairs along the main wall. The scene was complete with a reading lamp, end tables, and a TV stand—absolute luxury.

When I stepped inside, I squealed, and Greg lifted me off my feet in a massive hug. If anyone else saw the room, they might point out the untrimmed windows and lack of flooring, but, for us, kicking back in our leather chairs, we only saw the finish line. And it was just ahead.

What about You?

- Greg and Denise encountered so much, yet their neighborhood saw a united front. How could you present a better united front as a couple?

- Greg allowed Denise her desire to have a subcontractor work on their fireplace. He had been pretty intense about doing everything himself, but he knew he needed to let go here for her. The ability to be flexible, even if it is in small things, can help keep a marriage growing. What ways do you flex for your spouse? Does it make a difference?

Chapter 12

RESTORED!

*I*N LATE SPRING OF 2019, Greg had his workbench and tools set up on the piazza. It was midday, and he was trimming out the front windows.

A short, wiry man walked past the courtyard, and Greg called out, "Lucas, how are you doing? We rarely see you up on this end of Congress anymore."

Our former neighbor, Lucas, was a retired veteran with several tours in the Middle East. We'd heard he watched over our street. He was a man of character and advocated for all of us in the area.

He stopped and leaned with his hands between the wrought iron posts. "Nah, once we sold my mama's house a few years ago, I stay past Ashley Street." He wiped his face. "It's just plain hot."

Greg rubbed the end of his freshly sawn board to remove any stray bits of wood and then set it on the table.

Lucas stared at the house. "Man, this house looks like it's about done. It's gotta be five or more years since you started."

"Weekends and nights are all I've got to work, and I'm doing it all myself. We're at six years and counting."

"I'm over here to get a gyro from the Greek Festival before the long lines hit. The parking spaces are going fast, and the streets are crawling with visitors." He took in details about the house and smiled.

Greg said, "You got a minute to step in and take a quick look at what we've done with the place? Your gyro line is growing by the minute, but we can make it quick."

"Sure. I'd love to see it." Lucas flipped the clip on the gate and came up the steps in three lithe movements. He was small, wiry, and still in great shape.

He greeted me at the front door, then stood in a state of shock, taking it all in. We gave him a few seconds until he shook his head and said, "I was in here several times while the Smiths rented. Lordy, it's come a long way from those days."

Lucas took the tour. When he was ready to leave, he asked, as though this question had weighed on his mind: "Have you ever had anything stolen off your site in all these years?"

"I don't like to speak too soon for fear it might happen," Greg said, "but you know, I haven't."

Lucas laughed. "I guess those building materials under plastic in your courtyard are too heavy for them to carry off." He laughed, but what he said was true. It was too much work to carry off cement siding trim for quick money.

Greg nodded. "I try and make certain that things I store outside are not attractive to pawn shops. We also have a retiree on Carondolet who watches over all our houses and yards. He's called the police more than once if he sees anything out of the ordinary.

"Thanks for letting me come in and see your workmanship. You've restored her back better than new. Keep up the good work, man." He stretched out his hand for a shake.

Greg grabbed his hand and said, "Lucas, in those early days you warned us of men on our piazza who thought our house was abandoned. We have not forgotten your kindness. Stop by anytime. If we get that garden thing going again, I hope to offer a fresh tomato when you come by."

"Glad to help. It's so wonderful to see these Charleston Cottages restored and not torn down. It's people like you who make that happen." He turned to me. "Denise, you need to make sure he takes a break in this heat. And take some time to get you a gyro. I can smell those Greek potatoes from here."

Lucas swung the gate closed and tipped his hat. Greg went back to assembling window casings.

After Lucas left, I went back to my part of this project: sorting and folding laundry and Saturday's clean up, even if it meant a new layer of dust would surely fall by evening.

We planned to attend the Greek Festival on Sunday afternoon, not at its peak time. Passersby examined our house and whispered their opinions. I got a sense of how those in the heart of downtown felt with their homes on continual display.

With no real plan for the evening, we headed toward King Street where we could pop in and out of the eateries until we found two dinner spots. With 250,000 people attending the festival over the course of the weekend, we couldn't avoid the crowd.

Greg had taken a no-fuss shower, his third that day, and dressed in business casual. I wore my dark, skinny jeans and new loafers, a professional style that was comfortable for walking. We settled on a small bistro on the corner of Coming and Cannon. The building had the original sign for Wilhelmina's in the typical Charleston custom of preserving the past yet adding the new.

Greg ordered the mussels special, and I asked for their Thai hot bowl with ramen.

While we waited, he said, "The other night I came into the bedroom just to watch you sleep."

"What? Why? Was I drooling?"

"No. You were perfect. For once, you were quiet and still." He took a bite of bread and grinned. "Can't I just look at you?"

"It's just a little creepy to me . . . being watched." I chuckled self-consciously.

"This is me you're talking about . . . all my thoughts are good. Promise." He dipped his bread in the seasoned olive oil and casually said, "The zoning board has ordered us to tear out the deck."

My smile died. A harsher tone than I anticipated came out of my mouth. "What do you mean, tear it out?"

"They say it's too close to the structure next to us. It has to be a few feet away from their house."

"Even if their house sits on our property? We're not allowed to use the little bit of land we have left?"

"They said it didn't matter. Those are the rules."

"How long have you known this? You chose to tell me now when we're out for a relaxing evening? You've had time to process. Me, not so much." I crossed my arms and planted my elbows on the table.

"I know I mentioned this situation to you before now."

"I know," I said. "I just never thought it would end up like this."

"They sent me a letter earlier this week rejecting my plan." Greg turned his head to the side as if trying not to face me.

"Does that mean we can't have a roof to cover the back half of the yard? The afternoon heat is so intense; any outdoor furniture will be baked by the sun."

"Not within three feet of their structure, so I am thinking that's out too." Again, he turned away, almost as if he had let me down.

"We can't have a pergola or retractable awning? Ridiculous!" I removed my napkin from my lap and threw it on the table. My blood was boiling at the thought of tearing out our beautiful deck.

Then, Greg was glaring directly at me. "Just drop the subject, Denise."

"Drop the subject? You wait to tell me, and now we can't talk it through?" I felt the red rise up my neck. "I get sucker punched followed by tape across my mouth? Isn't that a tad unfair?"

"You have to push, don't you, Denise?" Greg

slapped the table lightly, letting me know he was dead serious.

I knew what I instructed my marriage clients to do in moments like this, but it didn't feel good. Greg was laying a hard line when I wanted a dramatic finish. This was the time when I was not to chase or pout but call a time out to regroup. Not my natural go-to. I didn't want this situation to end up in emotional separation. A deck wasn't worth it.

"Denise, I am warning you. Let's not embarrass ourselves here in public."

I put my head down and supported my temples with my hands. I breathed slowly, trying to regulate my response. *Why would he do this to me in the restaurant?* Did he do this to contain my reaction? I know I'm a handful, but why here? Now?

I closed my eyes, sighed deeply, and took a drink of cold water. I needed to dump the water on my head and let its coolness

CONSTRUCTION BREAK

An Exercise in Listening

If you no longer listen to each other and have little communication, it is not too late to begin again. Block out a chunk of undivided time and be realistic about what will be accomplished. Rules can include speaking calmly. If things get heated, point it out and return to a lower, less heated tone. Wise communication incorporates both emotion and reason in the exchange, but neither should take over. Purchase a small sample of floor tile from a local home improvement store. Sitting across from each other, take turns holding the tile. The person holding the tile "has the floor." The other is to let them talk it out. Allow each other to share the offenses that have chipped away at the foundation of the relationship. Allow both persons to feel heard. No excuses, no blaming allowed.

cover my body to contain the adrenaline. Several minutes passed.

"Greg, is there something else I should know?"

Weak from the first round, Greg opened the door a bit. "Nothing more than the usual stress at work, but the deck hit me hard. I wanted to add an inviting outdoor room. I've asked you to stop talking about it."

Actively listen to gain an understanding of what each of you has been going through. Both should have an adequate turn. Make a list of the heavy things you carry especially because of the other person. Most likely, these things come to mind when we consider how the other person grates on us. Once the list is made either verbally or physically, acknowledge that neither one can change what was. The only choice is to release these things and walk forward with the hope of more acceptable behavior. The balance is in understanding how much change the other person can make. Acceptance and realistic expectations are part of this process. When the offenses resurface, and they will, acknowledge that, together, you have chosen to release the offense, and you will not pick it back up.

Feeling like I was slapped, we ate in silence, payed our bill, and began the trek farther up King to a local bookstore. Usually we'd be walking hand in hand, but not tonight. Both of us were lost in our thoughts, attempting to make sense of the city's decision.

As we reached Cumberland Street, a tourist family stepped directly into my path and stood still, causing me to swerve to avoid hitting them. Without recognizing their intrusion, they turned their faces as though entitled to this bit of sidewalk, regardless of who they pushed aside.

I had no choice but to balance on the curb to get around them. Greg grabbed my arm as support while

I walked the ledge. His reaching smoothed my feelings, yet I knew a deeper talk was the only thing that would settle things between us. Greg wouldn't give me a quick recovery because he needed time too.

My anxiety grew on our walk to Buxton Books. What if he was tired of my insecurities? What if he was resentful of my constant pushing and lack of empathy?

In a few weeks we would celebrate thirty-two years of marriage. Surely, that milestone was worth something, but more and more I treated couples who'd been married much longer. They were dividing their lives and going it alone.

If we lost each other over this house, we'd lost everything. This project was not worth our marriage. I was constantly amazed at how quickly we could bounce from intense, close feelings to words that cut and destroyed in a moment's time. Thus far, we'd managed to come back together, but we were never beyond the heart breaking free from what binds us together. If that line was ever crossed, it would be hard to get back what was lost.

After nearly three miles of sidewalk, we returned to see that Gerry was on her step with a group of neighborhood friends around her. Her mother had passed away a few weeks before. A few days after we heard the news, I dropped in to see her. "What happened?" I asked to let her talk it out.

"She became quiet and didn't move around like normal about a week before we lost her. I called the doctor's office and scheduled an appointment, but she called to cancel. She was eighty-one, and I think she was ready to go. One day she was walking to Food Lion, and a few days later, she was gone."

"You took excellent care of her, Gerry. You took care of each other. I know life will be different. I'll miss her passing our house on the way to the grocery store."

As we came home from the bookstore, I saw on Gerry's face she was in that place where nothing worked right after an integral part of our lives was gone.

As we passed, I reached to take her hand. She rose to embrace me.

"Gerry, how are you?" I whispered in her ear. "I pray for you when you come to mind. I know you miss your mom. She always had a kind smile and word for Greg and me."

Greg nodded, his expression full of sympathy.

"Things will be a little crazy these first few months. Feelings of loss come in waves, but eventually they will become less and less."

Gerry squeezed me a little tighter. "I love you, Miss Denise."

"I love you too, Gerry. You know where we are if you need us." We released each other, and I started down the road, still looking back to her.

Gerry returned to her step. Family and friends said little, but their soft smiles said volumes. This was our neighborhood.

Our jagged emotions smoothed over, and we had a peaceful evening together. I stood on our deck, knowing he'd tear it out over the weekend to show the zoning board his intentions.

How quickly plans could change. So, we punted. Greg joined me with a drink and a stogie. This conflict opened a silent conversation between us with much said and less words.

The outside space was a loss for both of us. Amazing how the house evolved along with our own journey. When events spun out of our control, we had a choice in how we responded. We had to work with what was.

The next day, I was sitting on the floor trimming pictures. I was repurposing the original french door that used to close our front room at the fireplace. I had an affection for this door. It was the door I'd slammed when I saw the raccoon. It was the door I'd closed to keep out the dirt from the open floor system. It was the door that had put a boundary between us and the construction.

I painted the worn frame dark brown to mimic the rafters. Greg reglazed the glass to keep the panes from falling out. My plan was to use the mullioned windows as small frames for pictures of our house journey.

As I perused the photos, selecting carefully, I heard the key in the front door. I immediately braced myself. I hoped Greg was over our argument. I feared our disconnection right then. It wasn't like us to be this petty, but we'd never been under such stress for so long.

Even this close to completion, house projects still pushed us to the brink at times. I worried things were piling up between us. All of this swirled in my mind during those few seconds while I waited for him to come through the door.

Greg dumped the plans he'd been reviewing from work, his electronics, and other paraphernalia on the bar top. He leaned down low to kiss me. A man of few words, our connection was so much about these daily moments. After such hard words between us the day before, this day was anything but an ordinary rendezvous.

It was a picture of what I needed more in my life: time and space to stop, to just breathe, to feel I was not alone in this fight called life. Without Greg's insistence, my habitual busyness and multitasking would never have given me time to spend a moment of rest.

I was all about what I had to get done—namely dinner, dishes, and a general cleaning run-through—before I could pull out my book or laptop, filling a single twenty-four-hour day with way more activity than a sane person would ever consider. By that time in the evening, I found myself emotionally "touched" out.

When I continued my project, Greg touched my shoulder and said, "Denise, take a minute!" I read this as, *Please accept my apologies, and can we start over?* Still I lingered just a few moments more.

"This is my Denise-fix. You help everyone else, and right now I need your attention. I've craved this all day." He sat down next to me, waiting for me to set down the photos. I turned to melt into his arms. He hugged me like a man hugs a woman.

He wanted to take the weight of my day, and I let him.

Finally, I moved so he'd let go. "Come on . . . surely that is long enough," I said into his cheek.

"Just let me hold you. I was wrong in my defensiveness last night. I was discouraged and disappointed we lost the deck permit with the city. I took that out on you with my attitude. I should have told you about the deck."

"After all these years, you are still trying to protect me from what is happening? You should know I'd rather walk with you, so you don't bear the weight of this alone. It was unfair. All I want to do is to make everything better." I leaned back to observe him. "Are you sure you were only upset about the deck, or is there something else bothering you?"

Greg's face showed intensity. "Yes and no."

"What is it?" We faced each other, knowing this was important.

"You give everyone else the benefit of the doubt, but you are quick to question me. It's unfair to make your assumptions without giving me a chance. You keep believing I don't care about you when I give my life for you every day."

I remained silent. He was right. I poured out my life in every place but with him. Even if he was not completely ignored, he felt that way.

I reached out to hold both his calloused hands in mine. "When does this ever get better? Over thirty years, and we are still fighting the same battles." I brought his hands to my lips for a quick kiss. "You know you are my life, right? How can you not know that?"

"I do. It's what keeps me going." He looked at the

photos spread over the door. "What are you doing?"

"I am going through some of the highlights of our journey here thinking we could put the old french door on the wall like a big frame."

Greg began to look through the pictures. "I don't see a raccoon walking into the open wing. Oh yeah, you didn't get a picture of that did you?" He had a teasing grin on his face.

I giggled. "No, I sure didn't. Thank God!"

"I love the one of you leaning on the broom standing in the doorway with no floor in the kitchen."

"Yeah, that's a good one. So far, I have pics of the big stacks of flooring from James Island, the Habitat kitchen, your pickup loaded with a few thousand pounds of debris; Lord knows we did that trip often enough. Here's the moon shining down through the open roof and the end of our house torn off with James sitting on his bike chatting with us."

We fell into reminiscing. This no-closet, dusty cottage on the upper West Side of Charleston still pinged me from time to time but not so much anymore. My closet was clean. My pantry was organized. My washer and dryer hummed happily whenever I needed them.

This house will stand strong through hurricanes for at least a hundred more years. We've poured our heart and soul into her, raising her up to be the best she can be—strong and true. A fresh-faced beauty, she stands proudly on the corner of Congress and Carondolet. We love her for who she is, but more than that, we love her for who she helped us become.

What about You?

- In conflict, our first duty to our spouses is to examine our attitudes. Can we own our part in the hurtful exchange? Do you give your spouse time to evaluate and share after a fight?

- Consider how you might feel neglected in your relationship. Marriage does not meet all our needs, but we can be hopeful for growth in the holes that exist.

- Do you feel heard and understood?

- Can you lay down the desire to win the argument and find the value of two viewpoints? Where do you fall in on the logic/emotional curve? Are you moving toward a balance of logic and emotions because health lies somewhere in the middle?

Afterword

June 17, 2015

*O*ne Thursday morning about a year after Dawson's son died, I rolled out of bed and routinely switched on the coffeepot, then turned on the bedroom TV, muted, to the local news. Greg was catching a couple more z's before the day began.

"Greg!" I reached for the remote to turn up the volume.

He uncovered his head and sleepily blinked at the screen.

The female news anchor fought her emotions, trying to remain calm and professional as she reported that nine African American parishioners had been shot to death during a Wednesday night Bible study the night before. Police had little to go on regarding the perpetrator or his motive for the attack.

"Dear God, not here." I covered my mouth, trying to grasp something beyond comprehension. *Those poor families.* Tears began to flow. I grabbed a tissue.

Although yet unidentified, they had a video of a young white man in a Honda sedan. A nationwide APB was out to find the Honda, and a sketch of the young man came across the screen.

Greg pulled me up with him on the bed. He held

me tight while we wept for those families, for our community, and for our city. We prayed God's grace over those who were hurting and prayed law enforcement would find this man before he hurt someone else.

Greg said, "Our firm worked with Cynthia Hurd and State Senator Clementa Pinckney. They were both part of this group." He shook his head, deep sadness creasing his forehead.

Finally, I dried my eyes. I breathed to pull myself together. I had clients that day.

As we dressed, I asked Greg, "Do you think there's a danger of rioting?"

Before he could reply, my cell phone rang. My best friend offered us a place to stay if violence broke out.

Several other cities had come to violence in situations like this. If burning and looting started, getting out safely might become difficult, if not impossible.

Holding my hand over the phone, I asked, "Should we leave, Greg?"

In his typical, calm way, he replied, "We don't have a reason to leave yet."

I thanked my friend and promised to keep her updated.

Sliding his keys and wallet into his pockets, Greg said, "We know our community, Denise. We're going to trust God for our safety. It will be OK as long as they catch this guy quickly before he does something else."

Just after 11:00 a.m., my receptionist stopped by my office to tell me they'd caught the man. A woman had spotted his Honda in Shelby, North Carolina, and called the police. Dylan Roof had surrendered without incident.

Friday, at Roof's bond hearing, one by one, the grieving family members stood in court and said, "You took something very precious to me, but I forgive you. May God have mercy on your soul. Repent of your doings before it is too late." They spoke about how those nine people had taught them to stand in love and not in hate.

Sunday, our church pastor spoke of the tragedy and our need to join together in showing our support for these fellow Christians. He went on to say, "Christianity is the shining light of forgiveness in the face of such horrendous acts. These grieving families shot an arrow into the very heart of hate when they stood in forgiveness. For this, we as a community are grateful."

Churches across the city wept for the pain and loss, but they also wept for the love we all felt sweeping over Charleston.

And while there were pockets of unrest, the AME church asked for solidarity and tolerance in remembrance of their loved ones, and the city responded.

Sunday afternoon, Greg and I rode our bikes to the AME church to write condolences on their poster, lay flowers, and listen to their outside choir—to cry with our community and remember the lives lost. Someone had wanted to incite war by an act of hatred, but there I experienced a deeper love than I'd ever felt in my life.

A local pastor worked his way through the crowd, hugging and speaking to everyone he met. When he reached us, I said, "We live on the West Side and wanted to come down in support of your church and to stand with you in your loss."

He took my hand and placed his other hand on Greg's shoulder. "We are praying this will be used in the lives of those in our faith and in our city to resolve to come together—all peoples. What someone intended for our ruin will be turned for good in the lives of those left. Our brothers and sisters are with God." Tears dripped from my jaw. "Thank you for coming this afternoon. People are coming in from all over the world to offer love and support."

I reached in my purse for a fresh tissue.

Before he left us, the pastor said, "Have you heard they are holding hands across the Ravenel bridge on the bike-pedestrian path beginning around 6:00 p.m.?"

Greg looked at me. "Thanks for letting us know."

The pastor moved on, and I said, "Greg, what do you think? Should we walk the bridge?"

"Let's do it. This is not the time to be hiding out in our house. We need to stand with everyone to show that this has brought about stronger unity and more resolve."

An announcement on social media said organizers hoped for three thousand people, enough to span the bridge holding hands. Within minutes after we reached the crest of the bridge, a large crowd filled the pedestrian walk. Someone with a bullhorn announced a moment of silence and then several prayed aloud. We felt the crowd begin to move across the bridge in two lines. The line we were in was heading downtown, and the other line was heading toward Mt. Pleasant.

Spontaneously, the lines began to high five each other as they passed. Cars on the bridge honked, and passengers waved to us. Instead of violence, the evil intention of that young man sparked an outpouring of love, unity, and solidarity. Nothing was looted or burned.

The next weekend, our neighborhood gathered to paint doves on a stone wall, an outpouring of the Charleston Strong movement. I often pass this mural, and it reminds me that regardless what others do, we can choose how we respond.

We will always remember the sacrifice of those souls and honor their families who offered the gift of forgiveness and filled the city with love.

Our Construction Chronicle in Pictures

Upper: original house, side view
Lower, left to right: original house, front view;
our squeeky gate

Upper: Denise standing inside the construction area with an open kitchen floor

Lower, left to right: the fireplace repointed by the American College of Building Arts; Greg on his Canadian fishing trip

Upper: dorm room sectional

Lower, left to right: the moon shining into the back room of the house; the original fireplace

Upper: the dumpster overflowing with debris from the wing demolition

Lower, left to right: makeshift kitchen sink; the stove the night the raccoon came into the house

Upper: the day our end of the house was exposed to the world
Lower, left to right: the finished siding on Congress Street; the
side edition on Carondolet Street

Suggested Reading List

The following books have been pivotal in establishing my paradigm in practice as a marriage and family therapist. I highly recommend them for anyone wanting more in-depth information.

Cloud, Henry, and John Townsend. *Boundaries in Marriage.* Zondervan, 2002.

Gladwell, Malcom. *Blink: The Power of Thinking without Thinking.* Back Bay Books, 2007.

McMinn, Mark R. *The Science of Virtue: Why Positive Psychology Matters to the Church.* Brazo Press, 2017.

Pingleton, Jared. *Making Magnificent Marriages: The Official Resources Guide for www.relationshiphealthscore.com.* Marriage Improvement Tools, 2013.

Sternberg, Robert. *The Triangle of Love: Intimacy, Passion, Commitment.* Basic Books, 1988.

Thomas, Gary. *Sacred Marriage: What If God Designed Marriage to Make Us Holy More Than to Make Us Happy.* Zondervan, 2015.

Wagner, Larry. *Help Me Help Others: Practical Ways to Build Healthy Relationships.* Redemption Press, 2016.

About the Author

Denise M. Broadwater graduated with distinction from Columbia International University with an MA in clinical counseling. Mrs. Broadwater has training and experience in treating anxiety, depression, life adjustments, and other types of mental health disorders. Her experience includes working with individuals, families, and adolescents. She is a licensed professional counselor and has an M.Ed. in educational administration with several years of teaching experience. She began her counseling career as an MST therapist, working with at risk families and youth. She employs psychodynamic techniques especially early in the process, but also includes therapies such as CBT, Gestalt, ACT, and DBT when deemed beneficial for the client. Mrs. Broadwater is a Christian integrationist in her writing and treatment. Her private practice is in Mt. Pleasant, South Carolina.

Denise has been married to Greg Broadwater, the love of her life, for more than thirty years. She has three adult children and recently became a grandmother. Denise and Greg continue to live in Charleston, South Carolina, where she sings in her church choir. Besides writing, her other hobbies include quilting and, more recently, rowing.

Visit her website at www.DeniseBroadwater.com.

ORDER INFORMATION

MOUNTAIN VIEW PRESS

To order additional copies of this book, please visit
www.mountainviewpress.com
Also available on Amazon.com and
BarnesandNoble.com
Or by calling toll-free (855) 946-2555